True top produc~ have to ask, "Now what?"

As dramatic changes continue to reshape the housing landscape, short-sighted "survival" plans become quickly outmoded. That's why Wells Fargo is proud to present this special edition of Myers' timeless book of wisdom to our builder clients. Within these pages you'll find tried-and-true selling techniques and advice to help you enjoy ongoing business success — *without question!*

As a leading retail mortgage lender that can now be accessed through more than 6,600 banking stores nationwide, Wells Fargo remains committed to responsibly growing homeownership. And strong, purchase-focused relationships with our home building industry colleagues are at the heart of that commitment.

We believe that being the best means bringing out the best in those we work with. So we're here for you in all the ways that count, with new construction loan specialists who work where and when they are needed; effective, easy-to-use processes; guaranteed on-time closings, and quick approval decisions for your buyers.

Working together, we can ride the winds of change and maximize our combined sales potential in any market, winning season after season.

Brad Blackwell
Executive Vice President
National Retail Sales Manager

Greg Gwizdz
Executive Vice President
National Retail Sales Manager

Wells Fargo Home Mortgage is a division of Wells Fargo Bank, N.A.
© 2010 Wells Fargo Bank, N.A. All rights reserved. 01/10

EQUAL HOUSING
LENDER

New Home Sales In A Nutshell ...

The Sales Script Book

By Myers Barnes

New Home Sales In A Nutshell … The Sales Script Book
By Myers Barnes

Published by:
Myers Barnes Associates, Inc.
P.O. Box 50
Kitty Hawk, NC 27949
Phone: 252-261-7611
www.myersbarnes.com

Copyright © 2009 Myers Barnes Associates, Inc.

All rights reserved. This publication may not be reproduced, stored in a retrieval system, or transmitted in whole or in part, in any form or by any means, electronic, mechanical, photocopying, recording, or otherwise without the prior written permission of the Publisher.

ISBN: 978-0-9820957-0-6

Library of Congress Catalog Number: 2008908576

Printed in the United States of America
10 9 8 7 6 5 4 3 2 1

Dedication

To my son Hunter
Who teaches me that
marching to the beat of a different drummer
in pursuit of a goal is a good thing.

To my wife Lorena
You have shaped my heart.

To my Mom
For a life of unconditional love.

To God
I am blessed beyond what I deserve.

To the current Real Estate Market
You have challenged my assumptions
and cause me to reinvent.

TABLE OF CONTENTS

SECTION TWO

Foreword

Probably the biggest objection I receive from salespeople (and this includes managers) centers on the notion of using planned dialog when selling new homes to potential buyers. Repeatedly, salespeople want to battle, debate and argue with me that they do not believe in scripts.

To anyone who tells me that, I say, "You're delusional! Wake up and smell the competition!" If you're really convinced that you don't believe in using scripts to sell new homes, then you're misleading yourself. The truth is that you already have a script you follow. You just don't realize it.

Let's do a "be honest" here. Every time the buyer walks into your model home, you use the same greeting. Every time buyers tell you they want to go home and think it over, you use the same response. Whenever you go over a contract to purchase a new home, you repeat the same information to each buyer.

Whether you acknowledge it or not, your entire presentation is highly scripted, even if it isn't on paper. You say the same things every day in the same way. So, in reality, it isn't that you don't believe in a script; it's that you don't believe in someone else's script.

Do you know what a script is? It's the words in a document that map out what's going to be said and what's going to happen. The document could be a screenplay performed by an actor, a news report read by a reporter or a playbook memorized by a quarterback. A script can be a speech filled with promises that is recited by a political candidate or one delivered to students by a professor who is dying of cancer.

Festivities at your local fair can be scripted. Convention planners script the day's events. Wedding photographers script their shots. The President of the United States would not even think about holding a press conference without scripted remarks. Olympic contenders have their routines scripted, as do performers on the popular reality shows "Dancing With the Stars" and "So You Think You Can Dance."

The reality is that musicians, athletes, actors, corporate executives and anyone in a profession that pays six figures knows the importance of scripting.

I've always loved music and one of my favorite groups is the Rolling Stones. I've seen them in my teens, twenties, thirties, forties and now my fifties. During that time, I've found out something about Mick Jagger. He still can't get no satisfaction. For the last 40 years, he has made his living singing the same songs with the same lyrics and the same tunes to the same audience. Each of his songs and concert performances is a scripted, choreographed and rehearsed presentation.

As a professional speaker, do you actually think I awake on the morning I have to conduct sales training and say something like, "I wonder what I'm going to talk about today? Oh, what the heck! I'll just go out there and let it rip." I don't think so! You'd have me off the stage in a heartbeat demanding your money back.

How many of you recall your first day of selling real estate? Remember how nervous you were? Why? You were intimidated talking to strangers because you didn't know what to say. So, why aren't you nervous now? Through repetition, you've become comfortable with what you're saying, whether it works or not.

Scripting is a good thing. The true challenge you face in new home sales is not memorizing the words in this manual. The true challenge will be changing your belief system and forming new habits.

Picasso said whenever he needed to learn a new skill, he had to become perfectly comfortable being uncomfortable. Here's hoping this workbook cranks the heat up a few degrees in your comfort zone and you'll become uncomfortable enough to leave your status quo behind and discover the richness awaiting you in the world of possibilities.

Happy Sales,

W. Myers Barnes

Introduction

The purpose of this manual is to assist you in the sales process by making your sales conversation sound professional, convincing and knowledgeable. The scripts contained in this book reflect concise, real-life situations and actual dialogue that you can use to gain an immediate advantage and achieve more sales.

Before you begin, however, let's get the objections out of the way. I've taken the liberty of listing the most common objections I've heard from salespeople and my responses. Feel free to choose your favorite or you can "script" your own, in case you would like to battle, debate or argue with me about memorizing the scripts in "New Home Sales in a Nutshell."

Common Objections From Salespeople

Some of the scripts and dialogues will not work in my operation or they clash with my personality.

That's understandable, so use what's comfortable for yourself and for your business. Build your sales presentation on what's adaptable to you.

I'll sound too rehearsed when I talk with prospects.

Not if you take these scripts and personalize (and internalize) them. My goal in creating scripted dialogue was to give salespeople an easier, more efficient way to sell new homes. So, rework these scripts until you feel at ease using them. Eventually, the discomfort will go away.

I'm doing okay in sales without having to memorize scripts.

Words have power in them. They chisel away at our relationships, sway our emotions, shape our business, impact our actions, make us smile and alter reality. In the field of new homes sales, I believe that scripting is the vocabulary of success. The words I have used in the scripts are intended to transform your sales; but it's your life and if you're happy with your status quo, then you certainly have the last word.

These are not my words, yet you expect me to learn them word-for-word.

I jokingly tell salespeople, "Of course, they are not your words. It's my name, not yours, appearing on the front cover of this workbook. I ask that you to learn the techniques word-for-word first and then, through time and practice, adapt them to your own conversational style.

Several years ago a student approached me with a notebook of his favorite closing techniques. They were essentially the same techniques I had shared; however, after he had memorized the original ones, he rewrote and adapted the closing strategies to suit his selling situations and personality.

It is a lot of work to memorize scripts word-for-word.

I understand. I fought it, too; but think of the alternative. If you continue to do business in the same manner, what kinds of results can you expect? The obvious answer is that, if you continue to operate the same way, you can expect the *same* results. You must determine within yourself that you will pay the price to experience the success you deserve — and that price is *hard work*.

An effective strategy for learning is to thoroughly read, study and reread your scripts *daily*. Like a professional athlete, you must warm up prior to the event. Another technique for learning is to rewrite the scripts yourself, making them more natural (conver- sational) to your own speaking style. A third method is to record your scripts onto an audiocassette or digital recorder in front of a mirror. The benefit is that you can listen daily to the dialogues in your car, practicing while you drive to work. Finally, the most effective method is to role-play your scripts and dialogues with other pro- fessionals who are committed to success. This is called "simulated selling" and it works.

I don't have time to memorize these scripts.

What do you have time for? Watching television? Playing video games? Scoring a few rounds of golf a week? It's all about priorities. What gets your attention is what you decide is important to you at that moment.

We all have the same amount of time. Every day that we awake, we have a potential 24 golden hours in our bank. How we invest that time forms our future and becomes the string on which we hang our experiences.

Is this an intense challenge? You bet, but the payoff will move you into the ranks of the Super Achiever and out of the routine holding pattern that gets you nowhere.

Section One

1

Communication

Communication is how we share thoughts, opinions and information with others using speech, writing, visual signs and body language.

You communicate your new-home presentation with word—words that will paint a mental picture of your community, homes and homesites. The vocabulary you choose will either multiply your prospects' fears or bolster their confidence. Negative words generate negative images, while positive words will create positive images.

Listed on the left are some negative words you'll commonly hear in new-home sales. Avoid using these because they can induce fear and skepticism. Replace them with the words on the right, which evoke confidence.

When talking to prospects	To Inspire Confidence & Credibility—
DON'T Say This...	**DO Say This...**
Agent: Agent is threatening and provokes a negative thought.	**Representative, Consultant or Counselor:** To consult is to offer helpful advice and render service.
Buy: To buy is to give up security, which translates into money.	**Own, acquire, get involved:** People love to own. They DON'T like to buy.
Cheaper: Diminishes value.	**Less expensive, more affordable, best value, smart money:** Reflects savvy value consciousness.
Commissions: They do not like to pay your commission as part of the purchase price. They expect us to negotiate the commission.	**Fee for service:** Your service always outweighs the fee.
Contracts: Sounds stiff, formal, difficult and requires the service of an attorney before signing.	**Paperwork, agreement:** Suggests mutual under-standing.
Problem: Everyone has enough problems. Don't Complicate the sale.	**Challenge or situation:** We rise to the call of a challenge.
Cost or price: It always costs too much and the price is too high.	**Total value:** Equates with fair return for the investment.

When talking to prospects	To Inspire Confidence & Credibility—
DON'T Say This...	**DO Say This...**
Deal: "Make a deal" or "Get a deal" sounds shifty. May be too good to be true.	**Value or opportunity:** An investment that leads to a favorable result.
Down payment: A request for security (money). Indicates future payments.	**Initial investment:** The beginning of something positive.
Monthly payment: People fear incurring more debt and already have enough payments.	**Monthly investment:** Money toward value and profit.
Pitch or spiel: Carnival conman, carpet bagger.	**Presentation:** Introduce an opportunity.
Sell or sold: People do not want to be sold to and do not want you selling to them.	**Help them to own or acquire; Get them involved:** "Mr Smith, once involved as an owner, you will enjoy the benefits."
Sign: Never sign anything until checking with an attorney.	**Approve, okay, authorize, endorse:** "Mr. Smith, could you okay agreements, authorize the paper work and approve the order, Please?"
House: Cold and unemotional. A lifeless building.	**Home:** Memories, holidays, warmth, a haven.
Lot: Suggests a tiny parcel or small plot.	**Homesite:** Where they will make the most significant emotional investment of their lives.

When talking to prospects	To Inspire Confidence & Credibility—
DON'T Say This...	**DO Say This...**
PUD, development subdivision, tract: Never use industry jargon. All these terms have negative connotations.	**Planned community neighborhood:** A warm place to live. Brings up images of a lifestyle with family and friends.
Offer: Guarantees a negotiation and says, "Let's wheel and deal."	**Agreements, paperwork:** "Mr. Smith, do you have any questions before we begin the paperwork?"
Spec: The most negative industry jargon. Speculative represents "built for profit." You establish negotiation with this word.	**Nearly completed home or completed home:** Ground-floor opportunity.
Builder spec: Industry slang.	**Showcase home:** "Mr. Smith, our builder's showcase homes are concepts that allow you to witness the quality of construction and give you the opportunity to acquire a completed home."
Condos, units: Only an amateur would say unit. Represents cold, unemotional structures that are connected with apartments.	**Home, villa, or residence:** Pride of ownership.

When talking to prospects	To Inspire Confidence & Credibility—
DON'T Say This...	**DO Say This...**
Complex: The very connotation sounds confusing.	**Amenities or facilities:** "Mr Smith, let me show you the exciting lifestyle our recreational facilities/ amenities offer your family."
Standard: Implies commonness, blandness, the everyday run-of-the-mill.	**Included features:** Positions the ordinary to the extraordinary.
Upgrades, optional, extras: Such as hardwood floors, custom trim, fireplaces.	**Special or enhanced features:** "Mr. Smith, the special features that could be included are fireplace, granite countertops, etc."
Left: Suggests hard-to-move homes or homesites.	**Available or remaining opportunities:** Suggests a planned release, saving the best for last.
Monthly dues, maintenance fees: Has the same mental impact as paying taxes does.	**Monthly maintenance investment or contribution:** An investment toward the integrity of their home and community.
Ups, be-backs, lookie-loos and tire-kickers: These words are industry slang. Let your customer hear, "Sam, you're up," or "Jenny your 'be-backs' are here," and you will send prospects running out the door.	**Customer, opportunity, probable home buyer, guest:** Out business is the customer to whom we owe our success. Each one should be treated and greeted with respect.

When talking to prospects	To Inspire Confidence & Credibility—
DON'T Say This...	**DO Say This...**
Appointment: This suggests an extended commitment of time required from the customer.	**Set some time aside:** Always ask or suggest a small investment of time. "When can we set some time aside to discuss this?"
Decision: People fear making decisions because of finality and the potential for making mistakes.	**Choice:** Choice ushers in the thought that the customer has options. "Lets make a choice on the home of your dreams." Choice suggests unlimited options with no finality.
Think: Never ask a customer, "What do you think?" Psychologists call this imprinting. Ask a customer what he or she thinks and it's a subtle suggestion to go home and think about what they're getting ready to do.	**Feel:** Ask a customer, "How does this feel? How do you feel about owning this home?"

2

Meet and Greet

The first three to four minutes that your customers are exposed to your sales center or model home is a critically important time in the sales process. This is their first face-to-face introduction to your community, company and sales representative. Consider the following key points when planning the strategy you should use when you meet and greet prospects.

Customers Shop by the Process of Exclusion

Competition in new home sales is fierce. Your competitors are chasing the buyer, often tossing incentives in their pathways that can easily become roadblocks for you. Current statistics indicate prospects are visiting as many as 5 to 12 communities — and in some cases up to 20 model homes — before making their decision to purchase.

This means potential customers are in a hurry and are shopping by a process — the process of exclusion. They are looking for reasons to exclude — instead of include — you in their shopping process. Literally, because of the vast array of offerings and the time involved in visiting so many communities and model homes, prospects are attempting to cross you off their shopping lists so they can more quickly narrow their options.

Not All Prospects Are Friendly

Experts agree that most potential customers are uneasy about entering strange surroundings (such as a sales center) and they lack confidence when meeting a salesperson for the first time. The reasons for this are:

① **THE PROSPECT IS CONFUSED.** Visiting multiple communities, sales centers and model homes is a time-consuming process and may be confusing.

② **THE PROSPECT IS IN A HURRY.** A home is the single largest investment, and yet the prospect is still in a hurry to get it done and is, therefore, shopping by the process of exclusion.

③ **THE PROSPECT IS AFRAID.** He may have been over-whelmed or intimidated by another salesperson.

④ **PROSPECTS NEGOTIATE.** Many potential buyers believe a hardened approach is the first safeguard to buying. Remember, a truly serious purchaser may assume the role of "the reluctant buyer."

⑤ **PROSPECTS ARE INFLUENCED BY THE INTERNET.** Because buyers are highly informed today, they may view the salesperson as nothing more than a talking brochure. In many cases, they know more about your competitor, company and even your neighborhood than you do.

The Process of Greeting Begins in the First Few Seconds

All great salespeople understand prejudging is not pre- qualifying. Prospects don't subscribe to this philosophy, however. They have a tendency to judge the book by its cover. So you can expect that within the first few seconds, they are passing judgement on both you and your community. Therefore, you should:

☞ **Exercise a warm, professional greeting.** "Hi! It's a great day, isn't it?"

☞ **Give your name to get their name.** "My name is ___ ; and yours is___?"

☞ **Extend your hand.** At the same time you give your name, extend your hand, maintain eye contact and give a firm handshake.

☞ **Welcome them to the community.** "Thank you for visiting (name of your community). Please, make yourself at home."

After the initial greeting, you immediately transition to:

Super Achiever: "Are you out looking at new homes today?"

 The prospect's reply will be basically "yes" or "no."

Your strategy is to get them to commit to a definite amount of time and slow them down.

Super Achiever: Your strategy is to get them to commit to a definite amount of time and slow them down.

 If the prospect replies, "Yes"

Super Achiever: "Are you out looking at new homes today?"

Prospect answers, "Yes."

Super Achiever: "Looking at new homes is invigorating, isn't it?" ...or... "Looking at new homes is a thrilling way to spend a morning/afternoon/day, isn't it?" ...or... "What inspired you to be out looking for a new home today?"

Prospect might say, "Yes, it can be." ...or... "We just want to see what's out there."

Super Achiever: "Mr. and Mrs. Prospect, how much time have you set aside to visit our community/homes/ homesites today?"

Prospect might say this: "We have a few minutes." ...or... "We're in a hurry." ...or... "We are on our way home from church and thought we'd stop by for a quick look."

Super Achiever: "Outstanding! I understand what you're saying, and I promise to be brief. I'm sure you're going to want a brochure and some information regarding our prices, which I'll be happy to provide. May I take just a moment to share some quick highlights about our neighborhood, amenities, homes and homesites?"

If the prospect replies, "No."

Super Achiever: "Looking at new homes can be invigorating, can't it?"

Prospect could very well say, "No! It's draining!" ("No" can be a good thing. It means that they are tired and frustrated with shopping and are nearing the end of their buying process.)

Super Achiever: "Boy, you sound a bit frustrated!"

Allow the prospect to elaborate.

Super Achiever: "Wow! I hear what you're saying. It really has been frustrating. Let me see if I can fast-track this for you and make it easier. I'm sure you're going to want a brochure and some information regarding our prices, which I'll be happy to provide.

May I take just a moment to quickly highlight the location of our neighborhood, its amenities and our homes and homesites?"

 Prospect: "We have ____ minutes." ...or... "We're on our way to _____." ...or... "We're in a hurry."

Super Achiever: "Well, in that amount of time, I'll make sure you receive whatever literature you desire and that you see our homes/homesites/community. But first, let me take a brief moment to give you a quick overview of (community), its location, our amenities and our homes/homesites. Okay?"

The Prospect's Opening Maneuvers

Remember, your prospects are in a hurry, overwhelmed and apprehensive about the possibility of making the single largest investment of their lives. The following scenarios are opening maneuvers the prospect may employ, along with your caution-light tactical responses.

Caution-light Tactic

Caution-light tactic is a response you make to prospect's maneuvers that is designed to slow them down so you can regain control of the sales conversation.

Opening Maneuver #1 — The Market

 Prospect asks: "How's the market?"

Super Achiever's caution-light tactic: "Unbelievable! It's an unbelievable time to be considering a brand new home. And here's why. We have a stunning selection and availability of homes/homesites and our builder/ developer has aggressively priced the homes/ homesites to create a compelling value. In addition, interest rates are at an all-time low and the financing terms available today make home ownership extremely affordable. It really is an unbelievable time to be shopping for a brand new home!"

Prospect says: "What about what I read in the media? They say the housing market has crashed."

Super Achiever's caution-light tactic: "Ms. Prospect, normally the media is representing national statistics. What's being reported does not apply to our marketplace and/or to our neighborhood."

Opening Maneuver #2 — The Incentives

Prospect asks: "What kinds of deals or incentives are you offering?"

Super Achiever's caution-light tactic: "I'm glad you asked! We offer impressive homes, a wonderful location, an incredible school district, fantastic customer service and we are an Energy Star™ builder. As you can see, we have a lot to offer! Not only that, when you find a particular home you want to own, we have some tremendous financing incentives as well."

Super Achiever's caution-light tactic (emphasizing incentives and one-of-a-kind homes/homesites): "We offer no incentives that apply across the board. Instead, our incentives differ from home to home. They can be a substantial amount, yet they will vary based on the particular home/homesite you choose and the time frame you need for moving. The first step is to select a home you really like and then we can discuss the incentive as it applies to that one-of-a-kind home."

Opening Maneuver #3 — Just Looking

Prospect says: "I'm not buying today. We're just looking."

Super Achiever's caution-light tactic: "Of course, you're not buying today! You don't have enough information to make that kind of a decision, do you? My job is to give you good information that will help you make a smart and informed decision. So, let's do this, shall we? Let me give you the information you need to make an intelligent choice and then we'll see how you feel at the end of our time together… okay?"

Opening Maneuver #4 — Brochure

Statistics reveal that 75% of all brochures that are handed out indiscriminately end up in a trash can within 24 to 72 hours. Remember, people shop online, but buy on-site normally after a personal visit to their one-of-a- kind home or homesite.

Prospect asks: "Do you have a brochure?"

Super Achiever's caution-light tactic: "I do … only I don't keep any information packets prepared ahead of time … and here's why. We customize our sales packets based on each individual home buyer's needs. Tell me exactly what you're looking for in a new home/homesite and I'll be happy to put together a new home package that you can take with you. It will include all the information you specifically want and you can review it at your leisure. Come on in and I'll have you back on the road in about five minutes with the package in hand."

Opening Maneuver #5 — In A Hurry

Prospect says: "We only have a few minutes. We're in a hurry."

Super Achiever's caution-light tactic: "I understand. Many of our best customers who have become happy homeowners said exactly the same thing. Since you are in a hurry, let me give you a fast-track overview to save you valuable time."

Opening Maneuver #6 — Just Shopping

Prospect says: "We have just started shopping."

Super Achiever's caution-light tactic: "Great! Congratulations! Then you have come to the right neighborhood first. I can equip you with good information, show you our amenities and homes and then you can use (community's name) as the standard of measure while you evaluate the other communities you'll shop. How does that work for you?"

Opening Maneuver #7 — I'm Not Alone

Prospect says that a spouse or significant other is remaining in the car.

Super Achiever's caution-light tactic: "Let's walk out to the car and include your husband/wife/significant other/family in a quick 60-second overview and perhaps that will inspire them to come in and share this experience with you."

Here's why you don't simply hand prospects a price sheet. The New Home Sales process requires customers to select their one-of-a-kind home or homesite. They must select a one-story or two-story home on a cul-de-sac or streetscape in your community. Regardless of which one they choose, it must be down to the "One and only one."

Opening Maneuver #8 — Price List

Prospect asks: "Do you have a price list?"

Super Achiever's caution-light tactic: "Mr. or Ms. Prospect, the reality is that we simply do not have a printed price list. That sounds strange, doesn't it? I know that's not what you're used to hearing. So, let me tell you why we don't. It has to do with price and availability. Invariably, with real estate, what you see today may not be available tomorrow. And we never know when the builder/ developer will be adjusting prices. But let me tell you what I know today. Our homes/homesites currently range from $___ to $___. Is that the investment range you were considering?"

If they answer that it's not a comfortable range, reply with: "How much are you considering?"

You may also say the following when the prospect requests a price list:

Super Achiever's caution-light tactic: "Mr. and Mrs. Prospect, I'll be happy to assemble a brochure for you; however, I will not be including a price list … and this is why. As shown on our community map, the red flags indicate sold properties. In fact, our rate of sale is __ new homes/new homesites per week. The reason we do not include a price list is because whatever is available today will, in all probability, be gone tomorrow. Also, as rapidly as properties are moving, we never know when to expect a price increase. What I am going to include in your brochure is a list of the price ranges you desire, and then I'll call you periodically with the status of sold properties and price increases."

Additional Greetings To Use

 Multiple groups. When there are several prospective buyers at one time, then greet all the individual prospects with a group greeting. You are attempting to discover who, in the group, is a genuine prospect.

Super Achiever: "Hi, welcome to (community). My name is ___. As you can see, weekends are a busy time here. So, how about gathering around and I'll give you a brief group presentation and assemble some literature for those of you who are really interested in owning one of our homes today. Oh, by the way, who is interested in buying a new home/homesite?"

Agency disclosure. Agency disclosure is mandatory. Your entire strategy is complying with the requirements without complicating the process.

Super Achiever: "Hi! It's a great day, isn't it. Welcome to ___. My name is ___, and you are? Before giving you a brief overview, I represent the builder/developer. Are you familiar with the state of (your state's) agency disclosure form?"

The separating couple. Remember, in most cases, it takes both the husband and wife or significant other to render a decision. Sometimes, at the beginning or during your presentation, a couple may separate. You must keep them together initially to give them both a quick overview and to start them in the right direction before they begin to shop by the process of exclusion.

Super Achiever: "Mary, John, if, for just the first few minutes, you will both stick with me, I'll give you a quick overview of our community as well as the amenities and the floor plans our builders offer. After that, please feel free to make yourself right at home and explore at your leisure. Is that okay with you?"

Realtor immediately wants to gain control. Try a "be honest" approach. The cooperating broker has good reason to be defensive. It's his or her customer and s/he has every right to want to maintain control.

Super Achiever: "Welcome to ___. My name is ___, and yours is?"

The Realtor will either verbally identify herself or hand you her card.

Super Achiever: "Thank you, Ms. Realtor. It's good to meet you, and your customer's name is_____? Welcome, Mr. and

Mrs. Customer. You are very lucky to be with Ms. Realtor. By reputation, she is one of the finest professionals in the area and you are fortunate to have someone as knowledgeable to assist you.

"I'm sure you both are in a hurry, so I'll quickly tell you about our location, amenities and homes/homesites. Then I'll give you a customized new-home package complete with all pricing information and floor plans. After that, I'd like to invite you to take all the time you want to view our homes. Please feel free to explore them on your own, making notes of any questions you might have for me … or, if you prefer, it would be my pleasure to personally show you the home and community, pointing out the features and answering any questions you might have along the way. How would you be most comfortable?"

A Lesson From Lincoln

Abraham Lincoln's strategy for winning a debate was to determine the issues of the counter-party in advance. From there, he would develop his questions and answers and then present the case from their point of view.

To be a Super Achiever, follow the strategy practiced by our 16th president. Prepare your questions and answers in advance so, when the time comes to stand before the prospect, you will be organized, equipped and confident.

3

Qualification

The fact is that you simply cannot conclude a sale with unqualified prospects. They must have the money, desire or need to own, and the authority to purchase, all within a reasonable time frame. Focusing on serious buyers — not serial lookers — is crucial to your success, whether the economy is bust or booming.

Current sales research shows that as many as two-thirds of today's presentations are wasted on individuals who are not qualified to purchase. How can this happen? Because salespeople are delivering their presentations from the wrong point of reference. They are telling prospects what *they think* they want to hear, which is probably based upon the salesperson's personal assumptions rather than facts.

Before your presentation begins, you must do a "needs assessment." The best way to find out what your prospects need and want is to ask them. Sigmond Freud said that if you question carefully and listen attentively, every person will tell you how to help them.

Super Achiever: "Before I can help you look, I need to know what you're looking for in a new home. So, do you mind if I ask you a few simple questions before we begin?"

As logical and sensible as it seems to prequalify a buyer, most salespeople still fail to do so. As a result, they end up discouraged and frustrated, unable to understand why they are having a difficult time closing a fair percentage of their sales.

Consequently, your first **priority and continuing mission** throughout the sales process should always be to align your presentation with the emotional and financial motivations that will cause the potential home buyer to acquire your home.

How do you do this? You walk your prospects through the five categories of qualification.

The Five Categories of Qualification

① **Area.** By survey, the number-one consideration your prospect will have in shopping for a new home/new community is **"the area."** Regardless of how dazzling your presentation is or how your community shines, prospects will not own in a (geographic range) that does not fit their values and emotional agenda.

> **NOTE TO SELF**
>
> *For resort and retirement communities, my "hottest prospect" are those who have previously visited and/or repeatedly visit in my area. The habitual visitor is already sold on the location.*

☑ For year-round communities, the distance to work, school district, shopping, medical facilities, church and synagogue are the top priorities in the prospect's mind.

☑ In resort/retirement communities, the challenge may magnify. You must first determine if your state is right for them, as well as if they prefer the mountains, coast or inland communities.

② **Time frame.** How urgent is their need or how soon can the appropriate person(s) take advantage of your offering? *Time frame and financial resources normally will coincide with one another.* In other words, if a prospect says he is 90 days, six months or a year into the future, you will find there is a condition — such as selling his home — that prohibits the immediate sale.

③ **Financial resources (money).** Your prospect may want or need your offering, but if your homes/homesites are not within his financial parameters, then start searching for qualified prospects. If financial terms are required, you will need to further qualify your prospect in two separate categories:

☑ Down payment/initial investment

☑ Monthly payment/monthly investment

④ **Wants, needs, desires.** Wants and desires are emotional, while needs are logical. Because we are emotional beings by nature, we always want more than we need. Remember, what they want may not be what they need, which, in reality, is what they can afford.

⑤ **Authority.** Will you be able to follow up, secure and deliver your presentation to all those who will be involved in the *final* decision to purchase? Traditionally, when couples bought a home, there were always two people involved in the decision. Times have changed, however, and it isn't uncommon for there to be one decision maker — a wife, husband or significant other — buying a home. Just remember to make your presentation to everyone who might be involved in the decision-making process. In the case of a multicultural home buyer, the decision may not involve both the husband and wife. For more information on how to sell to multicultural home buyers, refer to my workbook *"Savvy Selling to a Multicultural Market."*

Qualifying — Area for Year Round Homes

Super Achiever: "Bill, Mary, let me give you a brief description of our community. As you see by our map, we are located (geographically). You will notice we are only a few miles from the elementary school district, a few minutes from the area's best shopping, with churches/ synagogues and medical facilities nearby."

"While we're looking at this aerial photograph, can you show me where your home is located?"

"Why are you considering moving to the area? (and/or) Why are you considering a new home? Are you looking to relocate to a better school district? Do you want more shopping conveniences or to move closer to where you work? Are you moving to get into/out of the city? Has your family situation changed (getting married, having children, downsizing, aging parents moving in)?"

From your area map, you would then progress to your community map and create an immediate sense of urgency.

> **NOTE TO SELF**
>
> *My best prospects are those who have either visited or vacationed in my specific state, county and/or town. This means the first sale (area) is made. If they are unfamiliar with my area, I must make two sales. First, I have to sell them on the area and , second, on my community.*

Super Achiever: "Mr. and Mrs. Prospect, before discussing our amenities, you will notice the homes/homesites that are tagged/flagged in red on our community map. This indicates those that have already been sold. As you can see, we are quite busy at (community). As a matter of fact, we have ___ homes/homesites that are purchased daily/weekly by families/people just like you."

You may consider pausing for a response, or continue with…

Super Achiever: "Mr. and Mrs. Prospect, you are going to love (community). As you can see by the number of homes/homesites that have sold, we are a popular community. We tell all of our customers that it isn't a question of whether or not *they will fall in love* with our community/homes/homesites. It's really a matter of, once they **do**, will we have what they are looking for because the homes/homesites are selling so quickly?" … or… "Once they do fall for our community, will we be able to have their new home built as soon as they need it?"

Qualifying —Area for Resort & Retirement Communities

 Prospect: "We are just beginning to drive the coast."

Super Achiever: "Bill, Mary, let me give you a brief overview of our community. As you notice by our aerial map, we are located in (state.) As you drive the coast, you will have several states from which to choose. Have you (A) narrowed your choice of states and (B) decided whether you would prefer being in the mountains, inland or on the coast?"

From your aerial map showing the states, you would then progress to your town map and locate your medical facilities, shopping, etc. From the town map, you would progress to your community map to create urgency and present your amenities.

②

Qualifying — Time Frame

Time frame is critical and is a consideration that normally coincides with financial resources. If prospects say they are looking far into the future, it is normally because of a financial condition such as selling their current home, acquiring the initial investment or anticipating a retirement or inheritance. All are events that may block an immediate sale.

To get a true picture of what time frame your prospect is working within, follow one of the following scenarios:

Scenario #1

Super Achiever: "Ms. Prospect, how soon are you thinking of making a move?" ...or... "How soon before you invest in your new home/homesite?" ...or... "How soon before you plan on moving into your new home?"

Prospect: "Probably six months."

Super Achiever: "Really! What will be different then?"

Prospect: "I will have sold my home." On the surface, she seems to be unqualified; but continue to explore.

Super Achiever: "I'm curious. Is it that you need to sell your home or you would just feel more comfortable if you sold your home first?"

Prospect: "I would just feel more comfortable."

By probing, you may have taken what initially seemed an Unqualified prospect and helped her realize her own qualifications. Keep going.

Super Achiever: "I guess what I'm asking is, if you found the perfect property at the ideal price, would it be necessary to wait until your home sells or would you take advantage of the right opportunity if it came along today?"

Prospect: "If it were the right opportunity, I guess I could move."

By asking a few more questions, you have taken what initially seemed an UNqualified prospect and proven to yourself and to her that she is qualified.

Scenario #2

In the event that the prospect says she must sell her home first, then proceed with the following script:

Super Achiever: "Ms. Prospect, I'm curious. Is it that you *must* sell your home or would it just feel more comfortable if you sold your home first?"

Prospect: "I have to sell my home first."

Continue to further qualify the prospect.

Super Achiever: "I understand. Have you listed your home?"

Prospect: "No. I haven't gotten that far yet."

Super Achiever: "Okay. May I make a suggestion? I know several Realtors who have a reputation for working one on one with homeowners who want to sell their homes before buying another one. How would you feel about letting me schedule a convenient time for you to meet with one of them to discuss your home's market value and the time frame you want to work within?"

Scenario #3

Prospect: "Unfortunately, the value of my home isn't what it used to be. So, I'm kind of hoping the market will improve and I can get more for my home if I wait."

Super Achiever: "The only problem with that is that, while you're waiting for your home's value to increase, our homes will also be increasing in value. So, although you may sell your home for more, you will probably pay more for a new home, too. In addition to that, mortgage interest rates will be going up. This will directly impact the overall cost of homeownership and may even place a new home out of your reach. It's a double whammy! Not only will you pay more for a new home, but your monthly payments will be higher because interest rates will increase.

"If you stop and think about it, you are living in a historical time to buy a new home. For the first time in decades, we have low interest rates and low prices. Normally, the scenario has been low prices and high rates or low rates and high prices, but now you have the best of both worlds. So, why not take advantage of this historical time?"

Scenario #4

Prospect: "I'm not sure I can afford a new home until I sell my current one."

Super Achiever: "That's a valid concern and I can certainly understand your position. In today's market, there are many types of loan packages available for sellers in your position. So, if the only thing holding you back from buying a new home is getting financed while you still own your current home, I can recommend a lender who stays up-to-date on the most recent financial strategies and will sit down with you to review all your possible options."

Scenario #5

Prospect: "I'm still not certain. Maybe I should wait and sell my home first."

Super Achiever: "Ms. Prospect, there are only two considerations in regards to real estate and your investment time frame. The two considerations are price and availability. First, you can feel certain whatever is available today will probably be gone soon. Secondly, it's highly likely that the values of remaining homes/homesites will increase. I'm wondering, as you've gone through the process of shopping for a new home, have you noticed increasing values and diminishing availability?"

> ### NOTE TO SELF
>
> *Securing the appointment has several advantages.*
>
> *1. It allows me to sell a home prior to the bank visit on a contingency basis.*
>
> *2. It assures a continuing appointment with me.*
>
> *3. It temporarily takes my prosspect out of the market by forming a relationship with me.*

Qualifying — Financial Resources

When qualifying financial resources, many times buyers start with a preconceived notion of how much they would like to invest versus how much they will actually invest. In other words, willingness to pay and ability to pay are two separate issues. New home buyers initially shop logically, but they buy emotionally and seldom stay within their budgets.

To avoid being trapped between the two extremes and to nail down reality, employ these three simple phrases: **"and up to," "no more than"** and **"How did you arrive at that number?"**

Scenario #1

Super Achiever: "Mr. and Mrs. Prospect, what investment range are you considering with your new home/homesite?"

 Prospect: "About $275,000."

Super Achiever responds quickly and curiously: "Up to?"

 Prospect: "Maybe somewhere around $300,000."

> **NOTE TO SELF**
>
> *Once my prospects change their investment position, then I have learned their true investment range.*

Super Achiever: "But no more than…?"

 Prospect: "Well, I'd say probably no more than $325,000."

Super Achiever: "And how did you arrive at that number?"

 The prospect may say: "I've been prequalified." …or… "It's a number that I'm comfortable with." Regardless, they have moved their position by $50,000.

Almost all prospects start out by telling you what sounds good; but what it should tell you is that they aren't revealing their true position. Using the three phrases will shepherd them a little closer to their actual price point. The philosophy behind this is that prospects don't want you to think they can afford as much as they can because they might be able to negotiate a lower price with you.

Scenario #2

The prospect may not change his or her investment range and may respond by saying something like this:

 Prospect: "There is no 'up to.' We are at $250,000. Period!"

Option 1/Super Achiever: "I understand. At the same time, not wanting to perform a disservice to you, if there were a particular home/homesite that was $10,000 to $15,000 more than your investment range, should I show this home to you or is $250,000 your absolute ceiling?"

Option 2/Super Achiever: "Mr. and Mrs. Prospect, our homes range from $___ to $___ and would require an initial investment of only $___. Have you set that amount aside or made arrangements for the initial investment?"

Qualifying — Wants, Needs and Desires

Your strategy is to help your prospects determine their hot buttons so, when you progress to the demonstration/site selection portion of the sales process, you only show properties that satisfy their emotional agendas as well as their financial parameters.

Super Achiever: "Mr. and Mrs. Prospect, would you mind describing the type of home you're looking for? For example, do you want a one- or two-story? Do you like an open floor plan? How many bedrooms and baths do you want?"

Listen attentively while the prospect describes his or her new home. However, the prospect may respond by saying, "We don't know." ...or... "We're just out getting ideas."

Regardless of the response...

> **NOTE TO SELF**
>
> *If I can get them to describe their existing home and what they want in their new home, I will crystallize the vision for all of us and know their "hot buttons."*

Super Achiever: "What type of home do you have now?"

Lead them into telling you about its features, number of bedrooms and bathrooms, kitchen, dining room, yard, etc. Often you will discover they want many of the same features again.

Super Achiever: "Your home sounds wonderful. May I ask if there is anything about your home that you would change or improve?"

Qualifying — The Internet Home Buyer

Visits are out. Encounters are in — and encounters can occur on-site or online.

> ### NOTE TO SELF
>
> *It doesn't matter how many visits a prospect has had to my model home or community. What counts are encounters. How many of those have they had?*

In the old economy, prospects shopped by the process of elimination. They would drive around, build their short list and eventually settle on their new neighborhood and home. In today's economy, new home buyers shop by the process of exclusion on the Internet. They build their short list and then visit only the neighborhoods they are seriously considering. In building a list of places of interest, they will have many encounters. Each time they log on to your Web site, it's an encounter. So they could easily have had 10 encounters with your new homes/homesites before you ever get the first opportunity to meet and greet them.

Without understanding that reality, however, prospects will usually say, "I'm not ready to buy today. It's my first visit to your community."

Your job is to demonstrate that, while this may be their first *face-to-face visit,* it is actually not their first *encounter* with the community because they have been to your Web site and viewed it online.

Super Achiever: "Mr. & Mrs. Prospect, modern research indicates that almost everyone begins the shopping process for a new home on the Internet before visiting model homes. How about you? Did you visit our Web site?"

Prospect: "Yes, actually, I did."

Super Achiever: "Wonderful! Then I guess you could say you are familiar with us, so this would be like your second visit, right?"

Prospect: "Well, I guess you could say that."

Super Achiever: "Did you see any floor plans or housing designs or homes/homesites you especially liked on our Web site?"

Prospect: "Yes, I did."

Super Achiever: "Did you use our mortgage calculator?"

Prospect: "Yeah, I played around with it some."

Understand this line of questioning. Today, most people use their computers to begin the process of shopping for a new home. If they have already checked out your Web site and they are now showing up on your doorstep, then your community has made it to their short list of "homes to go see in person." That's a good thing because it allows you to close the sale the first time you meet them.

Why? Because, in reality, it may be their first personal visit, but not their first encounter with your new homes or homesites. Their first visit was virtual; the second was actual. They have even admitted that this is their second visit. They were so interested that they selected a floor plan they liked and prequalified themselves with the mortgage calculator on the Web site. This is a highly-qualified prospect.

Qualifying — The Non-Committed Buyer

Often, you will have visitors who are just looking and are curious to see model homes. The tendency is to dismiss them as browsers and discount them as viable prospects. Don't make that mistake. Countless homes have been purchased by those "just looking." Once a spectacular design or amenity-filled community catches their eye, a great salesperson can convert the non-committed prospect into an eager, qualified buyer.

> **Super Achiever:** "Mr. and Mrs. Prospect, how long have you lived in your present home?"

Regardless of the answer, follow up by saying: "I'm sure it was a great investment. I'm curious though, knowing what you know now, is there anything you would change about your home?"

Allow the prospects to elaborate.

> **Super Achiever:** "How about your neighborhood? Has it changed and developed the way you originally anticipated?"

Once again, be quiet and let them elaborate. If they express discontent with what they now have, you are in a position to proceed.

> **Super Achiever:** "Mr. and Mrs. Prospect, the truth is that many people just like you are relocating to (community) for those very same reasons. Please allow me give you a quick overview and you will discover for yourself why savvy home buyers love living in ____."

Qualifying — The Authority

One of your first goals when you meet potential buyers is to quickly determine who the decision-makers are. Because of modern non-traditional relationships, this isn't always obvious. So, you have to delicately figure it out without using an in-your-face approach. A subtle way is to casually inquire who will be living in the home.

> **Super Achiever:** "Ms. Prospect, how many people will be enjoying your new home?"

> **Prospect:** "Four."

> When you're dealing with multicultural prospects, the person(s) in authority will vary. To know how ro respond to these situations, please refer to my workbook. **"Savvy Selling to a Multicultrial market"**

Super Achiever: "And who would that would be?"

Prospect: "My children and significant other."

Super Achiever: "How many bedrooms do you need?"

Prospect: "Four, I guess."

Super Achiever: "Your bedroom plus two children equals three bedrooms. How would you use the fourth room, as a home office, den or guest room?"

Prospect: "As a home office."

Super Achiever: "Ms. Prospect, we have two phenomenal home/floor plans that have four bedrooms and one would be perfect to use as a home office. Let's go take a look. Oh, by the way, when can we assemble everyone together to go see your new home?"

First-time Home Buyers

Frequently, the first-time home buyer may have a "phantom buyer" (parent, relative, friend, investor) in the background. In this case, the following script works well, especially if the phantom buyer is a Realtor or another expert offering advice.

Super Achiever: "You are fortunate to have someone knowledgeable to help select your new home/homesite. Let's set up a convenient time, around both of your schedules, to meet so they can experience first-hand why you are so excited about the opportunities at (community)."

Partners in Real Estate

This strategy is primarily for resort real estate where it's common for groups of investors to invest. However, you should beware that, whenever a partner (friend, investor, relative, etc.) is necessary, it's a sure sign of a financially unqualified prospect.

> **When you secure an appointment, realize the advisor will play a critical role in the final decision your prospect makes. Regardless of how much time you have invested with your prospect, you must start at the beginning and go through the entire sales process again.**

Your strategy is to determine the qualification of one buyer independent of the other.

Super Achiever: "Bill and Mary, I'm curious. If Jan and Mike were unable or not interested in owning this home after you all view it, would you be in a position to proceed forward?"

 Bill and Mary: "Yes."

Super Achiever: "Jan and Mike, if Bill and Mary were not interested in owning this home, would you proceed forward?"

 Jan and Mike: "I'm not sure." …or… "No."

From the onset, you know that if Jan and Mike fall in love with the home and Bill and Mary do not, you do not stand much of a chance of selling it. Conversely, if Jan and Mike do not like the property, then Bill and Mary are still viable prospects. If this is the case, you may consider separating the two couples. Often the disinterested or unqualified prospect can become a negative influence in the interested party's decision to buy.

4

Demonstration & Home or Homesite Selection

> We assume that, if potential home buyers are not golfers, we do not have to show them the golf course. If they are not boaters, we do not have to show them the marina. If they are not physically fit, there is no reason to show them the fitness center. We assume they would not be interested, but we're wrong.
>
> In fact, the opposite is true.
>
> When selling to the emotions, you are a dream merchant. By showing them the golf course, marina and fitness center, you allow them to become visionaries ... to see themselves in a better light.
>
> You are showing them a solid reason to learn to play golf, to go out and buy a boat, to live a healthier lifestyle and to exercise.
>
> So, don't sell yourself and your prospect short. Show your homes, homesites and amenities ... all of them.

The key thoughts to bear in mind with this phase of the sales process are the two unpardonable errors commonly committed in community sales.

Error #1 — Failure to ask for the order.

Error #2 — Failure to lead boldly and confidently with a follow-me attitude when you're demonstrating your selection of homes and homesites.

Remember, when it comes to your home/homesite selection, you are not to *show everything*, even though prospects often indicate that's exactly what they want to see. However, you know that would be too overwhelming. Why show them something they are not qualified to purchase? They should only see new homes or homesites that are based upon their qualifications.

Demonstrating Amenities

Demonstration: Differential demonstration. The Super Achiever sells the differentials (amenities) that separate her community from the vast array of offerings available to the consumer. She knows what makes it unique and she shows it.

The three keys to planned community sales are: 1) Amenities. 2) Amenities. 3) Amenities. The demonstration of the community is a process of focusing on the lifestyle the neighborhood offers.

Your customers choose to own in a community setting for emotional reasons and for their own personal satisfaction. They would choose your community because they perceive that it will enhance their personal and/or family's lifestyle.

Human beings process all information by their five senses: sight, smell, touch, taste and hearing. The demonstration of the community's amenities, homes and homesites is the most powerful part of the sales process because it taps into these senses.

The Demonstration is Always from Your Car

Sometimes a buyer will insist on following you in his or her own car. It is impossible to demonstrate your community and deliver your presentation in separate automobiles. (Remember your follow-me attitude.)

Prospect: "We'll follow you in our car."

Super Achiever: "Mr. and Mrs. Prospect, it's important that you ride with me. We have many exciting features and amenities with our community that your family will miss unless I personally show you. So, come with me. Let's all climb into my car."

 Prospect: "No, really, we will just follow you."

Super Achiever: "Well, okay. Then I'll ride with you."

Walk directly to their car and get in.

The Prospect Wants to View the Model Homes Unattended

Super Achiever: "Mr. Prospect, I sense that you would prefer to look at the models by yourself and I want you to feel free to do so at your leisure. However, I'd like to quickly show you the first model and give you a fast overview about the unique exterior and interior custom features we build into all of our homes. It won't take but a moment and then you'll know what to look for when you tour the models by yourself." (Inject your follow-me attitude.)

The Prospect Wants a Plat and Price Sheet to View Homesites Unattended

Super Achiever: "Mr. and Ms. Prospect, a lot of times people want to first view the homesites themselves, but without fail they come back confused and frustrated. Though our homesites are numbered, identifying the property lines can be a challenge at times. Also, you will need someone to give you a quick overview of the community's features and amenities. Why don't I take you out and get you started in the right direction? That makes sense, doesn't it?" If the prospect is obstinate and insistent on viewing the homes or homesites without your assistance, proceed with:

> *The psychology of follow-up is that the prospect must have a reason to come back or call back and the salesperson must have a reason to call back or invite back. It is vital to understand the strategy of withholding information. If you give out critical information, such as a price sheet, the prospect no longer needs your assistance and has no reason to come back to your sales center/model home. Remember the process of exclusion. Prospects are trying to cross you off their short list. Don't give them any reason to do so.*

Super Achiever: "Mr. and Mrs. Prospect, I'm excited to assemble some information for you; however, I will not be including a price list … and this is why. As shown on our plat map, the red flags indicate sold properties. As a matter of fact, our rate of sale is __ new homes/new homesites per week. The reason we do not include a price list is because whatever is available today will, in all probability, be gone tomorrow. In addition, as rapidly as properties are moving, we never know when to expect a price increase. What I am going to include in your brochure are the price ranges you desire, and then I'll call you periodically with the status of sold properties and price increases. How does that work for you?"

The Prospect Questions the Types of Neighbors Who Live in the Community

It is a violation of federal, state and local government and civil rights enforcement groups to answer specific questions concerning race, religion, and sexual or familial status. You must make sure not to violate the law while also remaining diplomatic and cheerful.

 Prospect: "What kinds of people (or what types of people) make up the neighborhood?"

Super Achiever: "Your neighbors are folks just like you and everyone is a satisfied customer."

If they persist or become specific, respond with:

Super Achiever: "Mr. and Mrs. Prospect, according to federal law, no one practicing real estate is allowed to discuss the ethnic, racial or age groups of a neighborhood. I'm sure you understand my position."

Brush the issue aside and continue forward. However, if they persist, your only choice would be to answer: "Mr. and Mrs. Prospect, I'm curious. Are you a member of any federal, state, local government agency, or civil rights group?" *If they are members, they must offer disclosure.*

Demonstrating Unfinished Models

Usually unmerchandised or undecorated homes will not show to the customer's expectations as well as a furnished home.

Super Achiever: "Mr. and Mrs. Prospect, the home you are going to see will not be furnished or have any accessorized items. We do this intentionally so that, as you walk through the home, you will be able to visualize how you might decorate it."

The following script should be used when showing both the unfurnished and furnished homes because it will cause your prospects to become emotionally involved. They can only get emotionally invested if they can picture themselves living in the home … preparing evening meals, reading a book by the fireplace, relaxing on the deck, watching the kids play in their rooms, enjoying the view from their second-story office.

Super Achiever: "Tell me, who's the chef in the family?" *The husband raises his hand.*

Super Achiever: "And what's your favorite dish?"

Prospect: "Well, I know it doesn't sound very masculine, but I love to make my grandmother's chicken and dumplings."

Super Achiever: "Great Southern dish! Do you make it with noodle or flour dumplings?"

Prospect: "Buttermilk flour dumplings."

Super Achiever, doing a sweeping gesture around the kitchen: "That's my favorite way of having it, too. Now, can't you just see yourself preparing your grandmother's chicken and dumplings and other favorite dishes in this kitchen?"

Prospect: "Yes, I can."

NOTE TO SELF

When I engage my prospects in casual conversation and evoke pleasant memories that relate to "home," they begin to feel more connected to and more emotionally involved with the new home. By listening and responding to them, I can help them "catch the vision" of living here.

Super Achiever: "Is there plenty of counter space for your condiments and spices? Is there ample cabinet space?"

Prospect walks around, opening cabinet doors and checking out the appliances. By now, he is emotionally involved in this house.

Continue to Demonstrate the Home's Other Qualities

ENERGY EFFICIENCY

Super Achiever: "Put your hand on this double-paned window and feel the energy efficiency. By the way, the windows are filled with argon gas between the panes. This allows sunlight in, but filters out ultraviolet rays. The benefit is that sunlight will not damage or fade your carpeting and furnishings." *If the windows tilt, then have the prospect open and close the windows.*

LIVING AREA

Super Achiever: "Tell me about your furniture. Where would you place your sofa? Where would you put your piano? Wouldn't this room look beautiful decorated for the holidays?"

THE MASTER SUITE

Super Achiever: "Where would you place your bed? Where would you place your dresser? The walk in closet will hold ____."

THE GUEST ROOM

Super Achiever: "Would you use this as a guest room?" ...or... "How could you see yourself using this room?" (Home office, exercise room, hobby room, playroom, game room, etc.)

NOTE TO SELF

Demonstrate! Demonstrate! Demonstrate!

Selling new homes is a contact sport.

Don't sit on the sidelines.

THE CHILDREN'S ROOM

Super Achiever: "As you can tell, all the bedrooms are roomy enough for your children to share a bedroom or they can each have one to themselves." *Conclude the sale* by having the children select their bedrooms.

THE GARAGE

Have the husband describe how he would arrange his workshop.

THE YARD

Super Achiever: "If this were your yard, how would you landscape it?" ...or... "Do you like to garden? The right corner of the backyard is an ideal garden spot because it gets full sun."

Selling Without Completed Homes

In some cases, you may not have homes that are completed and ready for occupancy or construction is handled on a "to-be-built basis." Then you must present the benefits of having a custom built-to-order home.

> **Super Achiever:** "Ms. Prospect, our customers have proven that, when given a choice between having a home built especially for them that's customized to their taste or having to settle for a house that has already been built, they prefer having one that reflects their style and personality. Don't you think it would be exciting to take an active part in personalizing the most important investment of your life? With the homes in (name of community), you would get to choose your color and type of carpet, wall coverings, kitchen appliances, exterior colors, etc., instead of having your builder do it. You brand new home will be built especially for you and you won't have to settle for someone else's taste."

Resale Homes

Your prospects may reveal they are also considering buying a resale. While it isn't your responsibility to talk them out of that, it is your job to help them analyze what buying a resale represents.

> **Super Achiever:** Respond curiously and in a surprised manner. "Really? Why would you want to own a used home?"

> **Prospect:** "Well, we've never gone through the building process before and, quite frankly, it seems like a hassle." ...or... "Because we think they're cheaper (or we can get a better deal)."

Super Achiever: "Mr. and Mrs. Prospect, in the short run, a **used home** may seem slightly cheaper, but a **brand new home** is infinitely less expensive, and I'll tell you why. With a brand new home, you receive a new home warranty. In fact, not only is the home warranted, but also the kitchen appliances, heating and air conditioning units, as well as every part of the home are, too. Isn't the peace of mind of having new warranties worth a little extra?

"In addition, you can take part in the carpet selection, wall coverings and have your brand new home built exclusively for you, rather than to settle for someone else's taste. Have you ever really thought of the advantages of a brand new home?"

Homesite Selection

If you have models, it's best to progress to the showcase homes first where everything is completed so the prospect can carry a vision of a home to the homesite you plan to show. This way, when you get to the unimproved homesites, you have the advantage of mental pictures working for you. They will carry the mental images with them to the homesite. But remember your qualification: **Do not show anything they cannot afford.** If the prospect's budget is for an interior homesite, do not show **waterfront**. However, you can satisfy their yearning for waterfront by showing convenient community **water access.**

Demonstrating Homesites: Establish Uniqueness ... Urgency

Let's begin with a little Q & A time.

Q: *What do you call a boomerang that doesn't work?*

A: A stick.

Q: *How do you overcome your prospect's indecision and procrastination?*

A: With urgency!

Q: *What do these two questions have in common?*

A: Indecision and procrastination are like a boomerang that is broken. There is no action. It can be frustrating to ask questions that require your prospects to make a decision, and they don't respond or they keep putting it off. It ends up being a one-sided conversation with your prospects offering no feedback.

> **Keep prospects sharply focused on what's unique about your community.**

Q: *So, how do you force the issue? How do you get them into a decision-making mindset?*

A: By building urgency. You lead your prospects to take action *today* by creating a firey sense of urgency that provokes and excites them. Urgency is the "bend" that converts a stick-prospect into a boomerang-buyer.

Q: *How do you build urgency?*

A: By convincing your prospects that the homesite they are considering is the *one and only one*.

Q: *What makes a homesite unique?*

A: Lots of things, including…

- ☑ **Location in the community.** The neighborhood's amenities, nearness to water/mountains/woods/playground.

- ☑ **Size of homesite.** It is oversized.

- ☑ **Corner homesite.** Normally larger, corner sites offer creative placement of home and driveway.

- ☑ **Cul-de-sac.** Preferred because they are off the road. Safer for children.

- ☑ **Small homesite.** Less maintenance.

☑ **Exposure.** Will the homesite offer sunlight, breezes or protection?

☑ **Elevation.** Highest lot in area. Great view from summit. Towering trees. Out of flood zone.

☑ **View.** Water view, golf views, mountain views or views of landscaped common areas or a protected reserve.

☑ **Vegetation and trees.** Enhances curb appeal, provides protection and shade.

☑ **Green areas.** Does it back up to protected areas, meadows, wetlands, wildlife habitat, bird sanctuary, water elements, community-owned green space?

☑ **Location to other homesites.** May be located next door to the most expensive home/homesite in the community, prestigious neighbor, etc.

☑ **Topography.** Is the lot level? Is there attracive vegetation? Does it gently slope toward the road? Are there ditches for good drainage?

☑ **Nearby conveniences.** Is the homesite near shopping, churches, military bases, parks, a famous landmark, mass transportation, accommodations for visiting relatives, excellent schools, museums? Is the area a cultural centerpiece?

Trial Closing Questions You Always Ask During Demonstration/Selection

Our brain is visual. It thinks in pictures. Therefore, you structure a series of questions that causes prospects to picture themselves living in the neighborhood and the homes.

"Can you imagine yourself living in (community)?"

"Can you see yourself living in this home?"

"Can you picture your new home on this homesite?"

Super Achiever: "Ms. Prospect, after everything you've seen here today, can't you just picture yourself living in this community?"

 Prospect: "I suppose I could."

Super Achiever: "Great! Then our next step is to select your home/homesite."

 Prospect: "Sounds good to me."

5

Objections

Generally, the purchase of a primary residence or resort/ retirement home will represent one of the *single, largest investment decisions of a lifetime.* Seldom will people make a purchase of this magnitude without having questions or concerns. Regardless of how impressive and complete your presentation is, the fear of making a mistake will cause your prospect to be doubtful and hesitant at some point and you will have to deal with those concerns before you are able to conclude the sale.

The most effective and efficient way of handling prospects' questions and concerns is to apply the "Law of Six."

The "Law of Six"

The **Law of Six** states that customers really have no more than *six* objections to owning in your community. Because objections differ from one community to another, your job is to discover what the six common objections are that you hear most often and to develop airtight responses to them.

Following are the two most common objections new home salespeople hear, along with scripts and dialogs demonstrating how you should respond to them. The objections are (1) "I want to think about it" and (2) "I need to check with my lawyer, accountant, banker or a third party."

PROSPECT: I WANT TO THINK ABOUT IT

"I want to think about it" or "I want to think it over" is the most common objection you will encounter. In the best of situations, under the most ideal conditions, you will hear this almost every time you try to close a sale. The problem with "I want to think about it" is that it's a broad statement and not narrowed to any one specific concern. You have not quite reached the final objection so you have nothing concrete to overcome.

By following this script, you will move beyond the vague generality of "I want to think about it" and get to the final objection.

PROSPECT: "I NEED TO THINK IT OVER."

Super Achiever: "Hey, I don't blame you. I would want to think about it, too. Buying a brand new home is a big decision, isn't it?"

Prospect: "It sure is and it isn't one I want to make quickly."

Super Achiever: "I completely understand that! What might be helpful is if I assemble some relevant information for you to take home that will assist in your decision-making process. Would that be okay with you?"

Prospect: "Yes."

Super Achiever: "Good. Now, to make sure that I include information that relates to where you are in making a decision to buy a new home, I'd like to ask you just a couple of questions. Okay?"

Prospect: "Sure."

In a very casual, conversational manner, ask these questions as you assemble the information packet.

Super Achiever: "First, you mentioned you love this area. Is that correct?"

Prospect: "Yes, I love the area."

Super Achiever: "Your impression of the community is favorable, right?"

Prospect: "Oh yeah! The community is wonderful!"

Super Achiever: "Now, what about the home/homesite? How do you feel about the one you selected?"

Prospect: "We really like it."

Super Achiever: "So, what is holding you back from making this home yours? You like the community, the homes/ homesites and the area, but you're still hesitant to move forward. Do you mind my asking if it's the price of the home/homesite or the financial arrangements?" Once you have gone this far and your prospects are genuinely interested, in all probability their reluctance to commit is rooted in a money issue. It might be the price of the home/ homesite. It could be that they need to sit down with a lender because they don't know if they will qualify to buy. Or it might be that they think a competitor's price is lower. To attempt to pinpoint the reason for their hesitancy, try the following techniques:

> **NOTE TO SELF**
>
> *Since "I want to think it over" is the most common objection I encounter, if I don't want to memorize the closing strategies word-for-word, maybe I am not serious about the profession of new-home sales and should consider another line of work.*

PROSPECT: "I WANT TO THINK IT OVER."

Super Achiever: "You impress me as a proactive decision-maker. Why don't you and I take the bull by the horns and reach a decision right now?"

Prospect: "I still need to think about it."

Super Achiever: "Why invest more time thinking this over? You have told me you love the area and can't imagine living in another community. We have selected your floor plan and you chose the perfect homesite. More importantly, it's within the parameters of your budget. Haven't you thought about it already?"

Prospect: "I just need to take more time to think this over."

Super Achiever: "I understand. Let's think out loud together and share with me your reasons for wanting to own in *community*."

Why should you push for a commitment from your prospects?

Well, you know they are interested. You have determined that they are happy with their choice of home/homesite. So, why wouldn't you try to close?

If you're reluctant to move ahead, ask yourself: If you give them more time to decide ... if they wait another week or so ... what will change? What's going to be different then that will help them make the decision to purchase in your community?

This is what will change. Once that normal sales cycle is broken, you will be history — and here's why. People are emotional beings. Each choice we make is flushed through channels of emotions before it ever drifts down the mental stream of logic.

The moment your prospect leaves your presence and community, the emotion is drained from the opportunity to own. You will quickly become a distant memory. It's likely they won't even think much about your homes after they leave because others will be getting their attention. (Remember that list they want to shorten?)

The majority will not even keep your brochure and literature, much less review it. What they will do is to move on with their lives. Therefore, the time to nail down the sale is during, or at the end of, your presentation when they have selected their home/homesite and just need a little nudging/encouraging/affirmation before closing the deal.

By taking the lead and helping them achieve what they truly want, you can save them from hours of indecision and from possibly buying a home/homesite elsewhere that they won't like nearly as much.

 PROSPECT: I NEED TO CHECK WITH MY LAWYER, ACCOUNTANT, BANKER OR A THIRD PARTY.

The second most common objection is one in which prospects say they can't close because they must check with someone else, such as a spouse, lawyer, CPA, business partner or whomever. The best response to this objection is to use the *"Subject To or Conditional Terms Contingency Close."*

Here is a scripted example:

 PROSPECT: "THIS SEEMS TO BE PERFECT, BUT BEFORE MAKING MY FINAL DECISION, I NEED TO RUN THIS BY MY BANKER (LAWYER, ACCOUNTANT OR A THIRD PARTY)."

Super Achiever: "I understand. Then am I correct in assuming that you are totally satisfied and there is no question in your mind that owning this magnificent homesite/home is the right thing for you to do?"

 Prospect: "Yes, I'm certain. I just want my banker to look it over."

Super Achiever: "Great! Then the only question is whether your banker says, 'It's the right thing to do.' Is that correct?"

Prospect: "That's it."

Super Achiever: "Mr. and Mrs. Prospect, may I ask you a question? (*pause*) Just suppose your banker was present at this very moment and she advised you to take advantage of this gorgeous home/homesite. Would you act today?"

Prospect: "I suppose we would."

Super Achiever: "Unfortunately, she is not with us today. However, prior to your speaking with her and to guarantee that someone else will not purchase your home/homesite, let's prepare the paperwork now and we will make the sale 'subject to' your banker's approval. This way the process has begun, we've secured your homesite and if, by chance, she doesn't agree, we will simply start over. That makes perfect sense, doesn't it?"

This is a powerful strategy for three reasons:

* By making the sale "subject to," you remove all risk.

* You "smoke out" the possibility of an Insincere objection.

* You take the prospects "out of the market," they cease shopping and have peace of mind that they have locked into the home or homesite they want.

6

Closing

A recent study conducted by a Harvard Business School professor revealed the number one reason that businesses failed. Do you know what that was? Well, it wasn't under-capitalization or poor management or even shoddy manufactured products. Although these can all contribute to a business failing, they aren't the main reason that companies fold. The primary factor that puts businesses out of business is the same one that will sink you ... a lack of sales.

How many times do you ask a prospect to buy before he or she says "yes?" According to statistics, salespeople have to ask for the order *five times* before they close on the sale.

Since it takes more than five attempts to make a sale, you need to stockpile multiple closing techniques that you have scripted, practiced and memorized.

Look at it this way. If you receive more objections than you have techniques, your prospect will always "one up" you, and you may never close the sale. Therefore, the reason you learn multiple techniques is to have more response methods than they have objections. Use each of their "no's" to lead them upward to "yes."

Picture this. Every "no" is a rung on the ladder of sales success. At the very top of the ladder is a new home sale. So, every time a prospect tells you "no," you step up a notch, hold on and stand firm until you get to the next "no" or, perhaps, a "yes."

You will find some ladders require many steps; others don't. What you're looking for is closure to the sale … whether it's a "yes" or a "definite no because I'm buying elsewhere."

One benefit in climbing the ladder one rung at a time is that every step gives you a better view of what lies ahead with your prospects. With each question and each "no," you learn a little more about what they want and where they stand. It also fortifies you for the next ladder … and the next prospect. For those of you who are hesitant to ask for fear of appearing like hard-sell, high-pressure salespeople, remind yourself that asking for the order is the fundamental character trait of top sales professionals. You probably are not going to have any prospects walk into your model home and say, "Hey, will you come over here and sell me a new home?" Therefore, if they aren't going to ask you, then you're going to have to ask them. If you do not take the initiative, you will eventually be out of business for lack of sales.

So, stop hesitating! Ask! Ask enthusiastically! Ask confidently! And continue to ask until you reach the top of that ladder and grab that new-home sale.

THE ORDER FORM CLOSE

This is a fundamentally successful closing technique. Why is the Order Form Close so effective? As you fill out the contract, you are not directly asking the prospect to buy (or make a decision). You are simply assuming the decision for him.

Begin the *Order Form Close* when the prospect asks a question that indicates a buying signal. You answer the question with a question of your own and record the answer on the order form.

Prospect: "How much is the down payment?"

Super Achiever: "Mr. Prospect, we require an initial investment of either 10 to 20 percent. Which one is better for you?"

Prospect: "I'd like to get in for the least amount, so I suppose 10 percent."

Super Achiever: "Okay. I'll make a note of that."

As long as the prospect does not stop you from recording the answers on the contract, he is buying. However, the prospect may stop you and say something like:

Prospect: "Is that a contract? You're ahead of yourself, aren't you? I didn't say I was buying anything."

Super Achiever: "Of course you aren't! I would never expect you to own without knowing all the facts. I use this form to write all the information down. It has everything about your home arranged in a precise manner. All the information both you and I need for our review later. That's okay, isn't it?"
Prospect: "Well, I guess so."

Super Achiever: "By the way, Mr. Prospect, if you were to buy the home/homesite you selected, we could schedule the delivery of your new home in 60 days, at the same time your other home goes to closing."

Every closing strategy is based upon the Order Form Close. This means you must be ready to close anytime and anywhere ... the moment your prospect says "yes." Keep your closing forms, calculator, pen and all other closing materials you'll need wherever and whenever you are with a prospect.

Prospect: "Actually, I would rather move my furnishings in a few days before my old home closes."

Super Achiever: "Fine. I will make a note that delivery must occur by the 25th of June. Would that give you enough time?"

Prospect: "Yes, that would work."

When you have asked all the questions and the contract is completely filled out, then review all the notes with the prospect. If he agrees with what you have recorded, ask him to authorize or okay the agreement.

The goal is to always get the prospect on paper. However, there are customers who are stubborn and will ask you to present a verbal offer to the builder without a check and a contract. In this case, you will stand firm in your position to only present a contract and check to the builder.

Prospect: "Rather than prepare the paperwork, can you first check with your builder and see if this is even possible?"

Super Achiever: "For any type of offer to be valid, consideration and an agreement are necessary. In other words, to have a valid and binding agreement, we need to prepare the paperwork complete with your request and the initial investment. Otherwise, your offer won't be considered. So, let's complete the paperwork and I'll present it today to the builder along with your deposit check, okay?"

Prospect: "We would be much more comfortable if you would simply run this by the builder first *verbally* and see where he stands. If it's acceptable, we can prepare the paperwork afterward."

Super Achiever: "In addition to not having a valid agreement, Mr. and Mrs. Prospect, without the paperwork and the deposit check, my builder would not even review your request. And without him looking at it, your answer is an automatic 'no.' However, if I present your request with consideration and an agreement, then possibly the answer would be yes or he'd give us a counteroffer. So, as you see, in order to move your request forward, we must prepare the paperwork first. Let's do that now, so I can present your request by the end of the business day."

This approach has the added benefit of being able to find out how serious your buyers really are.

THE YES MOMENTUM CLOSE

The purpose of this great close is exactly what it suggests. It consists of asking your prospects questions that lead them to answer "yes," thus building up the momentum for the final, "Yes, I'll buy!"

The goal of the *Yes Momentum Close* is to create an atmosphere of agreement. To do this, you first need to tie down the close by asking questions that, at the beginning or end of the sentence, solicit a "yes" answer. This approach psychologically ties your prospect into a "yes" mindset.

A List Of Tie-Down Words You Can Incorporate Into Your Questions.

Doesn't it	Hasn't she
Isn't that right	Won't they
Wasn't it	Aren't they
Couldn't it	Shouldn't it
Wouldn't it	Can't you
Aren't you	Don't you agree
Won't you	Isn't it
Haven't they	Didn't it

TYPES OF TIE-DOWNS

☞ **Deductive tie-downs** are the most common and are used at the end of a sentence to demand a "yes." *Example: "This homesite is a tremendous value, wouldn't you agree?"*

☞ **Inverted tie-downs** occur at the beginning of a sentence. These are less demanding and lead a prospect to say "yes." *Example: "Isn't it exactly what you had in mind?"*

☞ **Internal tie-downs** are used in the middle of your statements of fact. *Example: "Mr. and Mrs. Prospect, as we stand here on the deck, can't you just imagine how you and your family will enjoy this new home for years to come?"*

☞ **Tag-on tie-downs** are used to enhance value whenever your prospect offers positive statements. *Example: Prospect comments on how incredibly beautiful the views are and you add, "Yes, they are, aren't they?"*

THE TRIAL CLOSE

The purpose of the *Trial Close* is to evaluate and determine if you and your prospect are on the same page during the presentation. Since the best way to find out something you want to know is to ask, the best way to find out where your prospects are mentally and emotionally throughout your presentation is to ask their opinions. The answers they supply will allow you to gauge their readiness to own.

For example, you might say:

"Well, how are we doing so far?"

"Does this make sense to you?"

"Was this what you had in mind?"

"Is this what you are looking for in a new home?"

A *Trial Close* to memorize that will register the buying pulse of any prospect goes like this:

Super Achiever: "Mr. and Mrs. Prospect, on a scale of one to ten — with one meaning that owning may not make complete sense to you right now and ten being that it makes perfect sense — where are you on the scale?"

Prospect: "Well, I think we must be around a seven."

Super Achiever: "Great! I'm happy to hear that! What additional information do you need to help you get to ten?"

The benefit of the *Trial Close* is that prospects can answer honestly with a "yes" or a "no." Because you are testing the waters, their responses don't commit them or force you to end the presentation. They just give you a reading on how close they are to buying. Great salespeople use this closing strategy throughout their presentation to take their prospect's "buying temperature."

TRIAL CLOSES TO MEMORIZE

✸ "I sense you love this home/homesite. Am I correct?"

✸ "Can you see yourself living in (community)?"

✸ "What do you like best about this home or homesite?"

✸ "Tell me ... what is it about our community that most appeals to you?"

✸ "Can you picture your new home on this homesite?"

✸ "After viewing the features and benefits of our community/homes/homesites, wouldn't you agree it's unnecessary to even consider owning anywhere and anything else?"

THE INVITATIONAL CLOSE

The *Invitational Close* is a delicate, classy, yet powerful method that gently urges your prospect toward ownership. You can use this close when you are ready to conclude a sale after showing a home or homesite.

An *Invitational Close* will be preceded by a *Trial Close* such as, "Ms. Prospect, how do you like this homesite?" ... or ... "Mr. and Mrs. Prospect, can you see yourself living in this home?"

After asking the *Trial Close*, you issue the *Invitational Close* by saying, "Shall we make this one yours?"

Super Achiever: "Mr. and Mrs. Prospect, how do you like the home?"

 Prospect: "We absolutely love it!"

Super Achiever: "Great! Then shall we make this one yours?"

NOTE TO SELF

A rule of thumb: Never show a home or homesite without asking the prospect to own it.

When I do that, only one of two things will happen. Either the prospects will answer "yes," and I can congratulate them and move quickly to the Order Form Close and complete the contracts ... or the prospects will say "no" and I'll simply ask, "Why not?" Then I'll be very quiet and listen intently as they tell me what they are looking for in a home or homesite.

THE ALTERNATIVE CLOSE

The *Alternative Close* automatically concludes the sale by offering the prospects two or more alternatives. They have a choice between something and something or between something and nothing.

You never ask prospects, "Do you want this or not?" That allows them to say flatly, "No, I don't." Instead, you say, "Would you prefer item A or B?" Either answer is a "yes" decision ... "Yes, I want A" ... or ... "Yes, I want B." You record their answer on the paperwork and piggyback this strategy with the *Order Form Close*.

A. **Delivery:** "Ms. Prospect, closing could occur on the 30th of the month or the first of next month. Which would be more convenient?"

B. **Finances:** "We can secure your home/homesite today with an initial investment of only 10 or 20 percent. On this home, that comes to either $_____ or $_____. Which amount works for you today?"

C. **Appointment:** "I have either Monday or Wednesday available for this week. Which works better for you? Morning or evening? How about 12:00 noon for lunch ... or my next available time is 3:00 p.m."

D. **Included or added features:** "Which do you feel best complements your new kitchen? The oak or maple cabinets?"

THE SUMMARY CLOSE

When you approach the end of your presentation, the prospects are faced with arranging all the information they have heard into a clear, concise mental image before they can make an informed decision to buy. The *Summary Close* wraps up all the benefits you have pointed out and summarizes how your new homes/homesites and community meet their needs.

FOLLOW THIS FOUR-STEP PROCESS
TO DEVELOP YOUR *SUMMARY CLOSE.*

Step 1 — Bridge into your Summary Close with a transition statement.

"Ms. Prospect, we have covered a lot of territory today. Before moving forward, let's review the highlights of our discussion."

Step 2 — Reconfirm your prospect's wants, needs and desires.

"You mentioned (community) is ideally situated close to your work. Is that correct? And you're satisfied with the school district and the test-score ratings I provided for you, right? You said the amenities and security the community offers suit your lifestyle. Have I included everything?"

Step 3 — Summarize how the new home meets their wants, needs and desires.

"I'd like to suggest that we schedule an appointment with your lender to begin processing your loan and then meet with our design department so they can assist you in coordinating the custom features you want in your new home."

Step 4 — Ask for the order and close the sale (tie-down).

"The only remaining small detail is the preparation of the paperwork. I have taken the liberty of preparing the agreements in advance. All that's necessary is your authorization."

THE MONEY CLOSE

When a prospect says, "I need to think it over," it probably means that he is concerned about money. You can use the *Money Close* to break the financial terms into component parts that your prospect can understand.

Those three parts are: (1) total investment, (2) initial investment and (3) monthly investment.

Super Achiever: "Mr. Prospect, I sense your hesitancy. Do you mind my asking if it is the money?"

Prospect: "Well, actually, it is a little more than we anticipated."

Super Achiever: "I can certainly understand that, so why don't we take a look at the total picture and see if we can make some sense of it for you."

Total Investment: $ _____
"You feel comfortable with the value of our homes. Am I correct?"

Initial Investment: $_____
"Is that amount comfortable for you or is that amount readily available?"

Monthly Investment: $_____
"How does that work with your budget?"

By breaking the money into component parts, you can determine if your prospect's hesitancy is caused by the sale price of the home/homesite, the amount of his down payment or the money he must budget each month to cover his mortgage payment. When you learn the reason for his reluctance, then you'll know what's blocking the sale and you can deal with it.

THE REDUCTION TO THE RIDICULOUS CLOSE

This is also known as the *Calculate The Cost Per Day Close.* There is a world of difference between a prospect's willingness to pay and ability to pay. Use the *Reduction to the Ridiculous Close* to bridge the gap.

Whether the prospect's objections are "the competition will discount their homes;" "it costs too much;" "it's more than I want to pay;" or "I only have this much money budgeted," this closing method will easily overcome any money objection. How? By determining the difference in price and spreading the cost over a period of time.

For an example, suppose the competition is discounting their homes by $20,000 and your buyer asks you to do the same thing. How would you respond?

Super Achiever: "Let's review the $20,000 amount that you are asking the builder to reduce from the price. I sincerely appreciate your concern and $20,000 seems like a major amount until you break it down."

Hand the prospects a calculator and allow them to work through the math with you.

Super Achiever: At today's interest rates, for every $1,000 you finance, your monthly investment is $7. *(The number will change according to prevailing rates, of course, but the method remains the same.)* That means the $20,000 difference you seek is, in reality, $140 a month. Now, I realize that, at first glance, $140 per month seems like a lot; but break that amount down on a daily basis. In a 30-day month, the $140 becomes only $4.67 a day. Mr. and Mrs. Prospect, I bet you spend $4.67 a day on bottled water, a white mocha latte from Starbucks, a magazine or other inconsequential items, don't you? Well, for the cost of even one of these, you can own the brand new home of your dreams.

"I know this may seem ridiculous, but if you reflect on it, $20,000 isn't really that much over the long term. So, as a backup plan, if your offer is not accepted as presented, you're not going to let $4.67 a day stand in the way of owning the home you really want and deserve, are you?"

THE "NO" MEANS "YES" CLOSE

This strategy actually elicits the response all salespeople fear the most, which is hearing the word "No." With this method, you gently nudge the prospect into saying "no," *which actually means "yes."* Confused?

Here's how the *"No" Means "Yes" Close* works. Psychologically, the prospect is afraid of saying "yes." So, this allows the prospect to remain in her confort zone by saying "no," but it doesn't negate the sale. Instead, it takes a perceived negative ... which is no ... and makes it positive by having you assume or take for granted that the buyer is ready to commit. It's actually a positive approach. You will hear the word "no" in response to your question, but in reality the "no" is a "yes" because your question is, "Do you have any additional questions before we start the paperwork?" The buyer is saying basically, "No, I don't have any more questions, so, yes, we can start the paperwork."

Super Achiever: "Bill, Mary, it looks as if you have fallen in love with this homesite. Am I correct?"

 Prospect: "It's absolutely gorgeous."

Super Achiever: "So, can you see your new home on this homesite?"

 Prospect: "Yes."

Super Achiever: "Great! Do you have additional questions I can address before we start the paperwork?"

 Prospect: "No."

Super Achiever: "Wonderful! I'm thrilled to have you as part of our (name of community) family. I know you're going to love living here!"

> If the prospect had replied "Yes, I do have some questions," then your response would have been, "Great! What are they?" From there, you would answer their questions and, once again, conclude with, "Now that we've taken care of that issue, do you have any additional questions before we begin the paperwork?"

THE PLAN-B CLOSE

The *Plan-B Close* is rooted in the prospect's fear of loss. Although you have been encouraging a desire for gain by giving a brilliant presentation, the prospect may be hesitant and indecisive. So, rather than continue to speak in terms of the prospect's gain, you shift gears and now speak in terms of what the prospect will lose by not taking action.

Super Achiever: "Mr. and Mrs. Prospect, I can see you really love this home/homesite. Am I right?"

 Prospect: "Yes, that's right."

Super Achiever: "I also sense you are hesitant to make a commitment and you're having a hard time making up your mind. So, let me offer this suggestion. Since this is a popular community and this is the only homesite/home currently at this location/price/under these terms, it's likely that another buyer will come along and purchase your home/homesite before you do. Should this happen, let's have a Plan-B in place. Why don't we select a backup home/homesite that is almost as desirable as your first choice?"

The critical instruction: **Remain perfectly silent!**

 Prospect: "We don't want a home/homesite that's almost as desirable. We want this one."

Super Achiever: "I can certainly understand that. Then shall we move forward and make this one yours? The initial investment is only $__. Will you be using cash or personal check?"

This strategy *may not work 100% of the time. For instance, the prospect may respond with,* "We'll take our chances." … or … "If it's meant to be, it's meant to be."

Super Achiever: "Well, that sounds very accommodating, but there is also something to be said for going for what you want in life. Are you sure, if someone were to take **your** homesite, that would be okay with you and you would be willing to settle for something less desirable … something that falls a little short of being your ideal dream home/homesite?"

 Prospect *may now respond with*: "That is really pushy." … or … "We are just not comfortable going any further."

Super Achiever: "I understand. It's just that, in the past, several couples just like you have come back after a few days only to discover their homesites were owned by someone else. I don't want that to happen to you."

THE TAKE IT OR LEAVE IT CLOSE

Sometimes, to get closure, you have to offer a bottom-line solution and lay your cards on the table. That's when the *Take It Or Leave It Close* works.

Super Achiever: "The reality is, Mr. Prospect, that this home will sell … and it will sell at this price, under these terms and conditions. So, what you need to decide is if you will be the one to buy it. Unfortunately, it seems that we're in a Catch-22 situation. We can't move forward under the terms you are seeking because they don't reflect the true value of this home/homesite, and you don't want to buy it at the price set forth by the builder."

Pause for a moment, then continue: "Look, I'm a realist and I do want you to be comfortable with your new home purchase. In fact, I pride myself on not submitting the paperwork on a new home until the buyer is more excited about it than I am. Obviously, you aren't. So, the bottom line is that, if you're looking for discounts and concessions instead of a quality lifestyle and stable home values, then this community isn't right for you."

Super Achiever: "I can appreciate that you want the best price available and I respect that. By the same token, I hope you can appreciate that this isn't just the best price I can offer you ... it's the absolute lowest, take-it-or-leave-it price I can possibly offer you."

Another approach ...

Super Achiever: Mr. and Mrs. Prospect, I'll admit that not everyone can afford our new homes. That is a reality I have to face; and, if you're in that position, then please let me know and we'll focus on homes that are in your price range. However, if the sales price fits within your budget, then let's talk about value. Let's review what you'll be getting when you buy one of these new homes in this lovely community."

> **NOTE TO SELF**
>
> *I'd like to know more about how to close sales so I can increase my earning power this year. Buy "Closing Strong, The Super Sales Handbook" or one of Myers' other books on closing sales that are available at www.myersbarnes.com*

This may include the home's curb appeal, lot size, architectural style, infrastructure (water, sewer, sidewalks, tree-lined streets), community amenities, location, number of bedrooms, construction quality, builder's reputation and awards, appliances, "green" features, school-district desirability, neighborhood conveniences and proximity to water/mountains/beach/city/country/recreation.

7

The Best of the Rest: Additional Powerhouse Strategies

The world's highest paid sales professionals are those who are constantly practicing and rehearsing their selling techniques. Memorize these strategies and you'll boost your sales and your self-confidence.

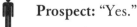 **PROSPECT: I DID NOT BRING MY CHECKBOOK.**

Super Achiever: "That's fine, but you say you would like to own and are prepared to proceed forward, except that you do not have your checkbook. Right?"

It is important you ask the question, to confirm if the checkbook is the only reason prohibiting ownership.

Prospect: "Yes."

Super Achiever: "I understand. Not a problem. In order for us to go ahead today and start the paperwork, any denomination of cash will serve as a good faith deposit and place a hold on this home/homesite. What amount do you have available today?"

PROSPECT: I DID NOT BRING MY CHECKBOOK AND I DON'T HAVE CASH.

Super Achiever: "That's fine, but you are saying you would like to own and are prepared to proceed forward, except you do not have your checkbook or cash available?"

Prospect: "Yes."

Super Achiever: "That's fine, I understand. We won't let these reasons prohibit ownership. Let's go ahead and prepare the paperwork and then I'll place your home on hold. Tomorrow morning I'll drop by your place or you can deliver a check to our office. What would be most convenient for you? Should I drop by or do you want to come to the office?"

PROSPECT: WHY SHOULD I CHOOSE YOU OR YOUR COMPANY?

The only way to answer this objection is for you to take the time to identify your strengths and differentiate yourself from the competition. I leave this one up to you. However, most consumers see a salesperson as a commodity. They feel we're all alike — one is the same as the other.

If you have not identified why a customer *would* choose you, then certainly the customer will be unable to understand why he *should* choose you, too.

PROSPECT: MAYBE I SHOULD WAIT TO CLOSE.

Sometimes referred to as the *Timing Is Not Right Close*. This is a perfect method to overcome procrastination or to uncover a smoke-screen objection. There are two ways to address "Maybe I should wait." The first is to answer the question with a question:

Prospect: "I'm not sure of the timing. Maybe I should wait six months?"

Super Achiever: "Maybe you should, Mr. Prospect. **However, may I ask a question?**"

Prospect: "Sure."

Super Achiever: "What will be different six months from now?"

Remain silent and listen for the concerns and final objections. It may just be a matter of offering concessions such as terms. Listen carefully and the prospect may reveal something minor you can overcome.

PROSPECT: WILL YOU DISCOUNT (CUT) YOUR COMMISSIONS?

Super Achiever: "I can appreciate why you're asking and I'll be up-front with you and say no. I will not adjust my fees for this reason. As a professional, my time has a certain value and I only work with people like yourself who realize the value of professional service."

Super Achiever: "Please do not think of what I earn as a commission. My earnings are based on a fee for service, and I can promise you my service will far outweigh the fee."

PROSPECT: WILL YOU ADJUST YOUR COMMISSION? YOUR COMPETITION WILL.

Super Achiever: "You're right, Mr. Prospect there are a lot of desperate representatives out there and I'm concerned. May I share why? We are talking about a person who doesn't even see the value in himself, and if he doesn't value himself, do you think he will value your business?"

PROSPECT: I WANT TO KEEP LOOKING.

With this close, you never argue, but congenially issue the invitation to shop.

Super Achiever: "Mr. Prospect, I understand you need to check other availabilities and prices. However, before you go shopping, I was wondering something: Are you the type of person who makes instantaneous buying decisions?"

Prospect: "No. That's why I want to shop."

Super Achiever: "Great! Then will you promise me something? Before you make your final decision, will you come back to see me? If you do, I promise you will receive the best value possible."

Prospect: "Sure. I'll not make the final decision without checking with you first."

Now, there's a chance the prospect is subconsciously committed to see you last. The idea that you may be able to offer a better value will entice the prospect back to you before rendering a final decision.

PROSPECT: I WANT MORE OPTIONS OR CHANGES IN THE HOME.

If the prospect asks for more options or a change in the home's features, you may respond by saying one of the following:

Super Achiever: "The more options we offer, the more complex our purchasing/building/manufacturing process becomes. Complexity adds to cost and that cost is reflected in the price of the home."

Super Achiever: "There are two terms or two points of consideration. One is *customization*, which involves structural changes that are not part of the home you selected. The other is *personalization*, and that is enhancing the home you have selected with personal touches. We only personalize with selections such as counter tops, floor coverings and cabinets that will make your home as unique as your own signature."

Super Achiever: "It's not a matter of price. It's a matter of how we build and the great price we are able to offer on the home. The plan you have selected is priced and value engineered "as is" and does not allow structural changes. I know this is not what you want to hear; it is, however, how **the home is priced, value engineered and offered for sale."**

Super Achiever: "I completely understand you want exactly what you want and that's very normal. The fact is that you're not going to get everything you desire, so you need to decide what you are willing to do without — at least for now. What you need to look for is the best home overall."

Section Two

8

THE PRACTICE OF POWER NEGOTIATION

① You are negotiating all the time.

② Everything you want or desire is under someone else's ownership or control.

③ Negotiating will not only help you get what you want, but will help you give others what they want.

> *Definition of negotiating:* **Negotiating is working side by side to achieve mutually beneficial agreements.**

THE UNDERLYING FACT OF ALL NEGOTIATIONS

Both sides want something. There is equal pressure and you should never approach the negotiating table feeling you are the only one who is in need. Both parties desire a specific outcome or there would be no reason to conduct the negotiation.

THE PREREQUISITES OF NEGOTIATION

Negotiation starts with intense preparation…all the work is performed ahead of time. The one who is most prepared is always the one who achieves the most favorable outcome.

①   Know what you want with absolute clarity. What is your desired outcome?

②   Know in advance what concessions you are willing to make.

③   Know what your options are. Can you live without it?

④   Know your counterparts and the subject matter.

⑤   Rehearse. Think through the process in advance.

KNOWLEDGE IS POWER

We all assume that other people want what we want and therefore attempt to conduct the negotiation in the same way we would. We all react and respond according to our own dominant personality style. Consequently, you should know yourself better than others do, and know others better than they know themselves.

Seek first to understand, then to be understood.
~ Steven Covey

PERSONALITY PROFILES

1 THE DIRECTOR

Directors are no nonsense, bottom-line people. Give them the ball and let them run. They like challenges and want immediate results. They love power, authority and prestige.

OBSERVABLE BEHAVIOR

First impression:	Direct and self-assured
Movement:	Quick and fast-paced
Main focus:	The task at hand
Priority:	Results….in the shortest amount of time
Irritations:	Wasting time, chit chat, and actions that postpone results
For acceptance:	Depends on leadership skills
Personal worth:	Measured by winning track record, results
Personal billboard:	"Notice my accomplishments."

STRENGTHS OF THE DIRECTOR	WEAKNESSES OF THE DIRECTOR
Born leader	Bossy, impatient, tactless
Unemotional	Comes on too strong
Embraces and is in dire need of change	Minimum tolerance for poor performance, mistakes and ambiguity
Goal oriented	Enjoys controversy
Well organized	Can't relax
Big thinker	Quick tempered
Thrives on competition	Big picture, but details unimportant
Excels in emergencies and usually has the right answer for a problem	May be right, but disliked in the process

2 THE EXPRESSIVE

The *Expressive* is a "people person." He or she likes establishing rapport, bringing people together and being natural bridge-builders. The Expressive is the type of person who would wear or drive red, and likes status and flashy possessions.

OBSERVABLE BEHAVIOR

First impression:	Open and direct
Movement:	Fast-paced
Main focus:	Relationships
Priority:	Open interaction, dynamics of a relationship
Irritations:	Boring task and being alone
For acceptance:	Depends on playful, charming nature
Personal worth:	Acknowledgment, being appreciated, personal recognition, applause
Personal billboard:	"Notice ME."

STRENGTHS OF THE EXPRESSIVE	WEAKNESSES OF THE EXPRESSIVE
Appealing personality	Too happy for some
Cheerful, upbeat, bubbly	A need to be liked by everyone
Sincere at heart	Distracted very easily
Adventurous	Talks too much and never gets down to business
Inspires others	Undisciplined
Charms people into ideas	Needs to be around people and be the center of attention
Makes friends easily	

3 THE AMIABLE

Amiable are slow moving but consistent, and enjoy helping others accomplish their desired results. They will consistently produce if conditions are perceived as perfect. They dislike change, because they prefer to perfect only what they are doing.

OBSERVABLE BEHAVIOR

First impression:	Open, warm, indirect
Movement:	Slow and easy
Main Focus:	Relationships
Priority:	Building trust and getting acquainted
Irritation:	Pushy and aggressive behavior
For acceptance:	Depends on conformity, loyalty and helpful nature
Personal worth:	Attention from others and acceptance of others
Personal billboard:	"Notice How Well Liked I Am."

STRENGTHS OF THE AMIABLE	WEAKNESSES OF THE AMIABLE
Low-keyed, easygoing and relaxed	Takes life too easy
Sympathetic and kind	Not goal oriented
Consistent life	Hard to get going
All purpose person	Can bring others down
Steady, dependable	Passive observer rather than active participant
Has good administrative ability	Resists change
Finds the easiest way to accomplish task	

4 THE ANALYTICAL

Analyticals love details and a standard operating procedure. They do not want to know what time it is, but rather how the clock works. They are slow to make a decision without analyzing every detail.

OBSERVABLE BEHAVIOR

First impression:	Self-contained, indirect
Movement:	Slow, steady
Main focus:	Task at hand
Priority:	Details and the process
Irritations:	Surprises, unpredictability
For acceptance:	Depends on accuracy and correctness
Personal worth:	Precision, accuracy, punctuality
Personal billboard:	"Notice my efficiency."

STRENGTHS OF THE ANALYTICAL	WEAKNESSES OF THE ANALYTICAL
Deep and thoughtful, purposeful	Spends too much time planning
Conscientious	Too meticulous
High standards	Not people oriented
Detail conscious	Prefers analysis to work
Lives by columns, graphs, charts	Dislikes those in opposition
Economical	Introspective
Analytical	Dwells on past negatives

CASE STUDY #1

Remember a Director May Want...

- ☑ Authority
- ☑ Challenges
- ☑ Prestige
- ☑ Freedom
- ☑ Varied activities
- ☑ Difficult assignments
- ☑ Logical approach
- ☑ Opportunity for advancement

HOW TO RESPOND TO THE DIRECTOR

➤ Provide direct answers, be brief and to the point. Confrontation may be necessary to gain their attention.

➤ Ask "what" questions, not "how."

➤ Stick to business.

➤ Outline possibilities for Director to get results, solve problems, be in charge.

➤ Stress logic of ideas or approaches.

➤ When in agreement, agree with facts and ideas, not the person.

➤ If time lines or sanctions exist, get them into the open but relate them to end results or goal.

CASE STUDY #2

Remember an Expressive May Want...

- ☑ Social recognition
- ☑ Popularity
- ☑ People to talk to
- ☑ Freedom of speech
- ☑ Freedom from control and detail
- ☑ Recognition of abilities
- ☑ Opportunities to help and to motivate others

HOW TO RESPOND TO THE EXPRESSIVE

- ➤ Provide favorable friendly environment. Never use confrontation if you want productive feedback.

- ➤ Allow Expressives to express their intuition and ideas.

- ➤ Provide ideas for transferring talk to action.

- ➤ Provide testimonials of experts on ideas.

- ➤ Allow time for stimulating and fun activities.

- ➤ Provide details in writing, but don't dwell on them.

- ➤ Create a democratic environment.

- ➤ Provide incentives for taking on tasks.

CASE STUDY #3

Remember an Amiable May Want...

- ☑ Status quo
- ☑ Security of situation
- ☑ Time to adjust
- ☑ Appreciation
- ☑ Identification with group
- ☑ Work pattern
- ☑ Limited territory
- ☑ Areas of specialization

HOW TO RESPOND TO THE AMIABLE

- ➢ Provide a sincere, personal and agreeable environment.
- ➢ Show a sincere interest in the person.
- ➢ Ask "how" questions to get an opinion. Allow for use of visual illustrations.
- ➢ Be patient in drawing out the goals.
- ➢ Present ideas or departures from status quo in a non-threatening manner. Give Amiables a chance to adjust.
- ➢ Define their roles or goals in the plan.
- ➢ Provide personal assurance of support.
- ➢ Emphasize how their actions will minimize their risks.

CASE STUDY #4

Remember an Analytical May Want…

☑ Security

☑ No sudden changes

☑ Personal attention

☑ Little responsibility

☑ Exact job descriptions

☑ Controlled work environment

☑ Status quo

☑ Reassurance

☑ To be part of a group

HOW TO RESPOND TO THE ANALYTICAL

➢ Prepare your case in advance.

➢ Provide straight pros and cons of ideas.

➢ Support ideas with accurate data.

➢ Provide reassurances that no surprises will occur.

➢ Provide exact job description with precise explanation of how it fits into the big picture.

➢ Provide step-by-step approach to a goal.

➢ If disagreeing, disagree with the facts, not the person. If agreeing, be specific.

➢ Provide many explanations in a patient and persistent manner.

CONDITIONS THAT CAN INTIMIDATE OR STRENGTHEN YOUR POSITION IN A NEGOTIATION

① **Home Court Advantage** ~ Negotiate on your home turf or in a neutral area. If you are on someone else's turf, you are out of your comfort zone and this alone can psychologically cripple you.

NOTE: The party who concedes this point is establishing a pattern for future concessions.

② **Fear of Titles** ~ From birth we are taught to obey parents, teachers, and those in authority. Titles conjure up feelings of authority.

NOTE: To reckon with authority, you must get away from the "title." When introduced to Dr. Bill Smith, or John Jones, Vice President, simply say: "Bill my name is _____. Is it OK if I call you Bill?"

③ **Promise of Reward** ~ Many times, when negotiating with those perceived to have social or financial advantages, you may allow them to have power. Beware when they start mentioning the yacht, plane, vacation house, etc. They are playing one-up-manship. Regardless of the outcome and promises, you probably never will be rewarded with anything other than that for which you initially negotiated.

④ **Fear of Punishment** ~ Also taught from birth, we are conditioned to fear failure and intimidation.

NOTE: To reckon with fear always be thinking, "What's the worse that could happen if my offer is rejected?"

⑤ **Control by Charisma** ~ It's fascinating how easily we are swayed by celebrity status or those who have high levels of personal charm. When you combine charisma with a title and you reward power, you can easily be overwhelmed. *NOTE:* The counterattack is to focus on the desired outcome, not the person.

DEVELOPING NEGOTIATION POWER

Before covering the tactics, there are *antecedents* to negotiating that must be understood.

The first is **emotion**. The more you are able to keep your emotions out of the negotiations, the more capable you perform. The key is not to get so caught up that you become overwrought.

Secondly, always appear as a **reluctant** buyer or seller. Perhaps one of the worst mistakes in negotiating is to give away your position when you become anxious, and appear to want what the other party is offering *too much*. The person who wants the least, gets the most; or better yet, the person who **appears** as though she wants it the least, gets the most.

Finally, regarding controlling your emotions and appearing as a reluctant buyer or seller, the skilled negotiator possesses "walk away" power. This means you must decide in advance that you are willing to walk away from the negotiation table all together.

If you ever feel so caught up emotionally that you are willing to give or take what the other side offers regardless of cost, you are not in a position to effectively negotiate.

NEGOTIATION TACTICS

The purpose of a tactic is to have the other person move from his or her position without moving from your position. As a professional negotiator, the tactics must be memorized so you not only learn their applications, but also how to deflect a tactic when it is used against you.

1. THE WINCE
An overreaction to the action of the counterpart.

They say the price is $350,000. You make a face (wince), overreact, and say, "$350,000! You're kidding!" Remain perfectly silent, and the counterpart now will defend or immediately drop his price.

Rule number one with application of the tactics is: *Never accept the first offer.* As a buyer, if the seller accepts your first offer, you will always feel you could have done better or something must be wrong. As a seller, you are left feeling you left money on the table.

COUNTER TACTIC TO *THE WINCE*

☞ Plan your concessions and always start high on price. By prearranging your concessions and knowing in advance how far you are willing to drop, you will still get what you want even if you end up at your ultimate fall-back position.

☞ Silence, and let the airwaves fill with concessions.

2. SILENCE
The most powerful tactic of all in a negotiation is the ability to remain silent.

The only pressure you are allowed to use in a sales presentation is the pressure of silence after you have asked a closing question.
~ Brian Tracy

Whenever you ask a closing question, shut-up. The first person who speaks, loses.
~ J. Douglas Edwards

COUNTER TACTIC TO *SILENCE*

☞ Silence.

3. OUTRAGEOUS BEHAVIOR
Surrendering to the counterpart's position by using fear as a tactic.

Unscrupulous and childish negotiators understand people will succumb to fear. Therefore, they practice *outrageous behavior* by slamming their notebooks, throwing their pencils across the room, or simply raising their voices.

Realize that the number one reason a negotiation fails is because both parties become emotional and an impasse results. **You cannot meet** *outrageous behavior* **head on.**

COUNTER TACTIC TO *OUTRAGEOUS BEHAVIOR*

☞ **Time out:** Side-step *outrageous behavior* by taking a break.

☞ **Set aside tactic:** "This is obviously a sensitive issue. Why don't we set this aside, discuss the other issues and return to this point later?"

☞ **Feel, felt, found:** "I understand how you feel. Others have felt the same way, but after consideration, here is what they found."

4. GOOD GUY, BAD GUY
A team tactic featuring a friend and an adversary.

With this tactic you have one team member who displays outrageous behavior toward the situation while the other party seems to remain neutral. After the *Bad Guy* displays outrageous behavior, the *Good Guy* steps in and woos you into believing he is on your side.

Beware of the counterpart who suggests to you, "I'm on your side, or I am working for you." Suddenly you have someone negotiating for you who isn't really on your side at all.

COUNTER TACTIC TO *GOOD GUY, BAD GUY*

☞ **Ask:** "You're NOT going to play *Good Guy/Bad Guy*, are you?"

☞ **Ask:** "Can you do this without (Bad Guy)?" If they are unable to help you themselves, then take a time-out until the person in authority is available.

☞ **Dismiss** the Good Guy, and only deal with the person who is in authority.

5. RED HERRING
A false trail, leading away from the true issue.

The *Red Herring* derives its name from the sport of fox hunting. Hunters participating unfairly would drag a dead fish across the path of the fox, diverting the dogs and sending them down a false trail. Skilled negotiators lead the unskilled away from the main issue by making a big deal out of insignificant issues.

COUNTER TACTIC TO THE *RED HERRING*

☞ **Employ the** *set aside* **tactic.** Say to the counter party, "This seems to be a major issue. Why don't we set this aside and establish agreement on the minor issues, then come back to this later?"

☞ If there is hesitancy by the counterpart to set the issue aside ask, "Is this issue your only concern? Since you agree there are other issues, I promise we can reach a mutually beneficial resolution if we come back to this later, after we have come to an agreement on a few of the minor issues."

6. LIMITED AUTHORITY
A final agreement cannot be reached without a third party approval.

Limited authority can be used twice in the negotiation process. In the beginning, when your counterpart may reveal he is in an information gathering stage and does not have the complete authority to render the final decision, and at the end.

COUNTER TACTIC TO *LIMITED AUTHORITY*

☞ Reschedule when all parties are available.

Limited Authority is more often used at the end of the negotiation. You have given the price or terms and it seems agreement has been reached until the counterpart says: "I need to run this by the committee, boss, wife, attorney, etc."

Counter by (1) Rescheduling until all parties are available. (2) Gaining commitment by saying, "I understand, but you will recommend they accept, won't you?" *or* "You can't make this kind of decision?!"

With *Limited Authority* as the negotiating tactic, the counterpart will now take your offer to the "nonexistent" committee and play good guy, bad guy. He'll then return and say, "I'm so embarrassed. I felt certain they would go along, and if it were up to me, I would accept. But, this is all they would agree to." (He now remains silent, waiting for a concession.)

Counter by withdrawing the offer. "Don't be embarrassed. I'm relieved. After consideration, I've discovered it would be impossible to honor my original agreement." (The other party will now defend his original agreement and you can play reluctant seller.)

7. FUNNY MONEY
Reducing price over an extended period of time to make the cost appear minimal and ridiculous.

The counterpart says, "Our product has a useful life of ten years so that's only fifty cents a day. You're not going to let fifty cents a day stand between what you really want and deserve, are you?"

COUNTER TACTIC TO *FUNNY MONEY*

☞ Multiply the aggregate over the period of time. Fifty cents per day over ten years is $1,825. Suddenly fifty cents per day is not a minuscule and ridiculous figure.

8. THE VISE
A tactic designed to clamp you in a seemingly immovable position.

There are three approaches with *The Vise:*

1) You'll have to do better than that.

2) Split the difference.

3) This is a limited offer.

1) You'll have to do better than that.

A rule with negotiation is whoever states his position first, normally loses. Rather than saying what he is willing to pay, the counterpart will get you to make a concession to see how far you are willing to go. Then he will respond with the wince, which will lead to another concession.

☞ **COUNTER TACTIC:** Respond, "How much better would that have to be?" (You get him to state his position, and then you wince.)

2) Split the Difference.

When you are asked to split the difference assume that, if you have the counterpart to the point where she is willing to split the difference, she will go further.

☞ **COUNTER TACTIC:** "What a shame we've come this far." Employ the walk away and revert to higher authority, which will allow you to reinitiate a new negotiation with the Good Guy/Bad Guy tactic.

3) This is a limited offer.

Never negotiate in haste. Successful negotiators realize there are no concrete deadlines.

☞ **COUNTER TACTIC:** If I have to make a decision *now*, then my answer is *NO*. However, if you can give me a bit more time, my answer may be YES.

9. THE TRIAL BALLOON
Presenting a hypothetical situation or solution to a challenge.

With this tactic the counterpart issues a hypothetical situation to see if he can get you to change your position. *Trial Balloons* are preceded by the following statements: Just suppose…I'm not certain…I may be talking out of school…I probably shouldn't mention this **but** what if I could…

COUNTER TACTIC TO *TRIAL BALLOON*

☞ If the counterpart issues a *Trail Balloon*, she is stating preplanned concessions. She has not reached her final position yet.

10. NIBBLING
Additions to agreement at the conclusion of the deal.

After the principal agreement is almost complete you hear, "Oh, by the way…" or "This will include_____, won't it?"

Your counterpart realizes that, out of fear, you have come so far and you don't want the deal to fall apart. You are at your most vulnerable state and may be willing to offer added concessions.

COUNTER TACTIC TO *NIBBLING*

☞ Say, "You've been grinding on me all day, you're not going to insult me by asking for more, are you?"

☞ You have successfully negotiated to the bottom line, and there's no more room.

☞ Use the *Trade Off.*

11. THE TRADE OFF
If I do that for you, what will you do for me?

Any time you make a concession, ask for one in return. This will elevate the value of the concession, and trading off stops the grinding away process. Your counter-part will eventually realize if he constantly keeps asking you for concessions, you will constantly keep asking him for concessions.

12. IN WRITING
Learn to negotiate on paper.

Don't think it. Ink it. Delegate to document, and when negotiating present any key benefits, warranties and assurances in writing. People naturally believe the written word over the spoken word.

COUNTER TACTIC TO *IN WRITING*

☞ "Where did that information come from?"

7 STEPS TO MOVE FROM AN IMPASSE

① **Start with the easy agreements first.** This builds a "yes" momentum.

② **Return to prior agreements:** "Look, we agreed on this and this and this…" "We've come so far. We're not going to let this stand between us, are we?"

③ **Take a hypothetical approach** and issue a *Trial Balloon* that causes your counterpart to look at things under a new light. "We've been talking about 24 months. 'Just suppose' I could extend the terms to 48 months?"

④ **Point out the negative consequences** of not reaching the agreement.

⑤ **Appeal to emotions:** "I really feel bad. We've had such a great relationship. I don't want this to come between us." (Silence)

⑥ **Call a time out,** and take a rest.

⑦ **Utilize the set-aside tactic.**

5 TIPS ON LISTENING

The ideal way to start any negotiation is with an interview type question. Such as:

"Ideally, if you could design the outcome of this situation, what do you perceive to be the best possible conclusion?"

You can initiate the concession process delicately by saying, "I'm sure this is worth every cent you are asking. It's just that I didn't realize it would be this much. Is there some way you could help me with the price?"

1. Hear your counterpart out and keep an open mind. Even if what she says in the beginning seems unreasonable, avoid a knee-jerk reaction and response.

Many times in the beginning we hear something which may not, at first, seem appropriate. Yet, by the time the counterpart finishes the sentence, paragraph or presentation, it may be *both* appropriate and acceptable.

2. Make a commitment and resolve to listen. God gave you two ears and one mouth, so use them proportionately. Question skillfully, listen attentively, and remember that if you let others talk long enough, they will tell you what you need to know.

3. Listen for facts verses feelings. Facts cannot be changed. Feelings are perceptions and may change.

4. Respond to questions with interest. You are seeking clarification so you can tip the information balance. Ask, "Why do you feel that way?" (or) "What do you mean?"

5. Eliminate Distractions. All competition to listening should be eliminated. Accept no interruptions such as phone calls and visitors AND KEEP YOUR DOOR CLOSED.

CONVERSATIONAL HINTS

☑ **LEGITIMIZER:** Honestly, frankly

☑ **ERASERS:** But, however

☑ **JUSTIFIERS:** I'll try, wish, maybe

☑ **DECEPTIONS:** I'm no expert, I'm just a country boy, In my humble opinion

☑ **THROWAWAY PRIOR TO A MAJOR ANNOUNCE-MENT:** By the way, As you are aware.

NONVERBAL COMMUNICATION — BODY LANGUAGE

Psychologists believe the spoken word hides more that it reveals. Words come from the intellect, and are, therefore, chosen and censored. Nonverbal behavior comes from the emotion and can more easily bypass our subconscious mind. Nonverbal behavior serves as a lie detector. After reviewing the following nonverbal messages, it will become evident that you should, at all costs, avoid negotiating by phone whenever possible. The adage, "Actions speak louder than words," can be a powerful tool in the process of negotiation.

Body language – Watch the face, eyes, hands, and head posture.

Face ~ Obvious and most expressive manifestations of a person's feelings. It reveals the emotions behind the word, and serves as true feedback for what is being spoken.

Rubbing eyes or ears with hand ~ May indicate doubt or lack of interest.

Stroking the chin ~ Shows thoughtfulness, consideration.

Pinching the bridge of the nose ~ Great concern or splitting headache.

Leaning back and supporting the head with both hands ~ Shows a feeling of superiority, authority, being at ease.

Rubbing the nape of neck ~ Frustration or tension.

Hand to mouth ~ Shock or astonishment.

Tugging at the ear ~ May mean the client may want to interrupt.

Placing of chin in hand and dropping his eyes ~ Boredom.

Hand And Arm Symbols

Strumming fingers ~ Impatience.

Clenched hands ~ Strong disagreement.

Two hands clenched together ~ Client is feeling intimidated and suspicious.

Wringing hands ~ Extreme anxiety.

Gently rubbing the palm with the hand ~ Shows expectation and delight.

oining hands in upward prayer-like manner steepling Indicates self-confidence and superiority.

Hands joined behind the back while standing ~ Indicates superiority or supervisory attitude.

Crossed arms ~ Protection and self-defensiveness. (Most important position in sales to be aware of. Your client is demonstrating he does not want to be involved with you or your offering, or he does not believe you.)

Posture

Leaning forward ~ Indicates they are interested. (You have their full attention and they could be ready for the close).

Leaning back ~ They feel threatened. (They are not ready to close. You must bring them back toward you).

Removing and cleaning glasses ~ To gain time or give thought.

Ear piece in mouth ~ They are trying to keep from speaking.

Eyes up while speaking ~ After asking a question, if their eyes go up, they are carefully considering the reply. If they are asking the questions and their eyes go up, they are carefully considering what they are asking.

Eyes and head go down ~ If you ask a person a question and the eyes and head go at the same time, you have a lie.

Planning to Negotiate

1. Study the *Negotiation* process and tactics thoroughly before beginning to plan.

2. Organize and reorganize and understand with absolute clarity what you are seeking to accomplish.

3. Prepare a written plan. When you write your plan of action, your thinking becomes clearer.

4. Think through the entire *Negotiation* process in advance. What kind of personality types are you dealing with? What is their agenda as well as yours? Move from your side of the table to theirs and think through how they will respond and react.

5. Plan your responses and have stock comments prepared. If you memorize the tactics and counter tactics you will always be thinking ahead of your counterpart.

6. Be concise and move quickly. Though preplanned concessions are important, ambiguity is not a part of *Negotiating*. If you indulge in steps one through five you will be prepared.

9

Scripts for Negotiating

The Fundamentals of Negotiation

① Before you begin to negotiate, you must first establish if your counter-party sincerely wants *to own* a new home or homesite.

② Verbal offers are worthless signs of commitment. **Commitment comes in the form of a check and a contract.** *When it's personal, it's important.* It becomes personal and important to your customer when you obtain a check and a contract.

③ In most real estate transactions, the customer wants to negotiate based on tradition.

④ Never allude that there may be room to negotiate. *If you are working for the seller* (developer, owner), *by law you are representing their best interest.* You are not a buyer's agent and the moment you negotiate for the buyer, you have crossed the line.

⑤ If, by chance, you are the listing agent, then price the property fairly in the beginning and prepare the owner for a firm-price strategy.

⑥ If you must make concessions, you only negotiate terms, conditions, closing dates, initial investment, etc. Never the price!

⑦ Negotiation is a mindset. Negotiation is a belief. *If you believe in the value of the new home or homesite, you will stay strong.*

Establishing the Strategy

Your strategy begins by gaining the prospect's commitment that he really wants to own a home or homesite.

Prospect: "We want to make an offer."… or … "What's the bottom line?" … or … "Do you think they will take less?"… or … "What's the best you'll do?."

Super Achiever: "That question sounds like you're interested in owning this home/homesite. Is that right?" … or … "Am I hearing you correctly, that you're ready to become the owner of this home/homesite today?"

If the prospect responds "no" to your questions, there is no reason to continue discussing price. Instead, flinch and say:

Super Achiever: "Really! Why not?"

Do not continue the negotiating process without your prospect's confirmation that he sincerely wants to be a homeowner.

The underlying fact of all negotiations is that both sides want something. You want them to become owners and they want to own your home/homesite. There is equal pressure so you should never approach the negotiating table feeling like you are the only one in need. Both parties desire a specific outcome or there would be no reason to conduct the negotiation.

Will You Take Less Than the Listed Price?

 Prospect: "We would like to make an offer." … or … "Will you take less than the listed price?" … or … "What's the best you can do?" … or … "What's the bottom line?"

Super Achiever: "That question sounds like you're interested in owning this home/homesite. Is that right?" … or … "Am I understanding you correctly? You're ready to become the owner of this home/homesite today?"

 Prospect: "Yes, but only if we can get it at the right price (or at a deal)."

Super Achiever: "Mr. Prospect, with today's technology, nearly everyone has access to a computer. In fact, the vast majority of new home buyers begin their search online. With all this information available at our fingertips, it isn't surprising that anyone can go online and find out how much you paid for your home. So, let me ask you something. How would you feel if you paid several thousand dollars more for your

> **CONTRACT POINTS**
>
> * If your contracts say "Offer To Purchase," change them.
>
> * Lose the phrases, "Let's make an offer" and "You will never know unless you ask."
>
> * Lose the phrase, "By law, I'm obligated to present any and all offers."
>
> * Lose the phrases, "This home is listed at $___," "This home is offered at $_____," and "The price they are asking is $_____."

home than your neighbor … and he knew it? The reality is that, if we indiscriminately offered different discounts to different buyers, everyone could know what everyone paid. This knowledge could not only breed resentment, but it would also affect property values.

"Mr. and Mrs. Prospect, are you familiar with how true real estate value is determined? In reality, the developer/builder or the salesperson representing the home/homesite does not determine value. Value is based on comparable sales. In other words, a professional appraiser says the property's market value is a certain amount based on recent sales of comparable properties.

"If someone purchased a comparable home yesterday for $350,000 and today you purchase the same model for $300,000, and tomorrow someone negotiates the builder down to $275,000, then what is the true value of that home?

"Mr. and Mrs. Prospect, we do everything we can to protect the values of homes within our neighborhood and, consequently, the equity in your home. If a brand new home is going to be one of your single largest investments, then isn't it reassuring to know that you are doing business with a builder who is concerned with guarding your personal equity and protecting the assessment value of the community?"

Super Achiever: "In many ways, a discount is really an admission of guilt by builders that they made a mistake and overcharged many other home buyers in the past. Now they're saying, 'We overcharged them at first, but this is what the home is really worth.'

"Beyond their admission of guilt, this pricing strategy is the fastest, surest way to insure a *meltdown* of your personal equity and the *meltdown* of equity in the entire neighborhood. You won't get that from this builder or this community. That's not how we do business."

This strategy is equally effective when negotiating with a buyer's agent.

We Could Have Bought (Months/Years) Ago for a Lot Less Money

Your strategy is to help them discover that their failure to act in the past will only cost them more in the future.

 Prospect: "We could have bought the same property for $___ last month/year."

Super Achiever: "You are not going to let that happen again, are you?"

If they say "no," proceed to contracts. If they hesitate, proceed with the following script:

Super Achiever: "What's important is not to focus on what you could have done in the past, but on what you will do in the future. Let's go ahead and secure your home/homesite today and next month/year you can sit back and realize you received today's best value in the time frame that was perfect for you."

The Competition Will Discount Their Homes

The strategy is two-fold and requires two scripts. In the first script, ask them why they haven't purchased. Though this is a bold response, obviously if it was a "deal," they would not be talking to you. In the second script, you want them to realize someone else's deal may not be to their true advantage.

SCRIPT ONE

Prospect: "Your competition is making better deals." … or … "Will cut their prices." … or … "Is offering substantial incentives."

Super Achiever: "Mr. Prospect, I do not want to appear discourteous, yet I'm puzzled. If you feel it's such a great price, why haven't you purchased one of their homes?" Remain silent and let them state their reasons, such as, they might like the homes but not the community, or they like the price, but not the designs, quality, etc.

Remain silent and let them state their reasons, such as, they might like the homes but not the community, or they like the price, but not the designs, quality, etc.

Super Achiever: "Mr. Prospect, it seems price is not the true issue. What you're really concerned with is obtaining the best value, is that correct? Let's take a moment to discuss what's truly the best value for your family and/or investment needs."

SCRIPT 2

Consider these scenarios:

Prospect: "I like your home, but the competition is priced $20,000 less." … or … "The competition is offering to discount their homes by $20,000."

Super Achiever: "I don't understand their business strategy! Mr. and Mrs. Prospect, why do you think they would do that?"

Prospect: "They are having a difficult time selling their homes." … or … "They need to sell their homes." … or … "Have you looked outside recently? There's nothing but for-sale signs up and down the street. Property just isn't selling, so I guess they want to do something to attract buyers." ... or ... "I don't know why and I don't care. I just know they are."

Here are some ways you can respond to their request for a discount:

Super Achiever: "May I ask a question, please? Is a brand new home one of the *single largest investments of your life*? Will you be making one of the largest investments of your life based purely on incentives or how much the home is discounted?"

Super Achiever: "Every builder wants to get the maximum selling price for his homes. Wouldn't you agree? So, are you really getting a discount or are you paying the maximum amount they can get? I ask this because, if you think about it, in reality the discounted price is all the home is really worth."

Super Achiever: "Are you comfortable with the thought that they are cutting prices and deals? I'm just a little concerned. Will you ever know if you got the best price or did someone else get a better deal than you did? And if they are having a difficult time selling their homes, will you be comfortable making the *single largest investment of your life* in a community where homes aren't selling? How will this affect their value long-term?"

Super Achiever: "Our builder knows what his homes are worth. He built value into these new homes from their blueprint conception. This builder has a reputation for not sacrificing superior value for quick sales. He didn't cut corners or use less-expensive materials so he could afford to reduce prices later when the market tightened. If he didn't discount his homes when they were under construction, why would he discount them now?"

We Can Get a Better Price Per Square Foot

The prospect may try to negotiate by comparing price per square foot with another builder.

> **Super Achiever:** "We have never looked at it that way. You see, there are so many variables — such as materials, warranties and customer satisfaction — when determining the price of a home. I'm curious. Are you looking for your new home based solely on price per square foot?"

> **Prospect:** "No, but we do want the best price."

> **Super Achiever:** "Great, then what you're looking for is the best value. Is that correct?"

> **Super Achiever:** "Settling on a square-foot price is difficult because a home's true value is not determined by square footage, but component parts, such as the materials in the home. Let me give you an example. The price of carpet is $___ per square yard, while tile is $___ per square foot. What we need to do is determine what you would like in your home and then we price the home according to the materials we use. That makes sense, doesn't it?"

> **Super Achiever:** "In searching for a new home, there are three points to consider: (1) Price per square foot, (2) Quality, (3) Service. Unfortunately, as a builder/developer, we can only deliver two of the three at the same time. Which two are you most interested in receiving?"

We Can Buy a Bigger/Larger Home From the Competition

The prospect may try to negotiate by stating the competition builds larger homes with less custom features than yours.

A **Super Achiever:** "Mr. and Mrs. Prospect, we don't just build what is known as a big-box floor plan with a lot of square footage at the cheapest price. Our commitment is to design custom features that reflect your personal taste and make your home as unique as your personal signature. We pay attention to craftsmanship, quality materials and life-long commitment to customer satisfaction. All things considered, if price per square foot and a big box is how you base your comparison, we may not have what you're looking for. Now that you understand our value is in the total package, can we take a few moments to discuss what features are important to you/your family?"

B **Super Achiever:** "Mr. and Mrs. Prospect, the basic big box you are considering may be an outdated plan. Let me explain. Ten years from now when you want to sell your home, if your floor plan is ten years old, then you are really marketing a 20-year-old home. Our designs are cutting edge, up-to-date and will carry forward, holding their value for years to come when it is time to resell.

"There are a lot of ways to cut price when building a home and a big box is one of them, but it is not forward thinking in this day and age. Let's discuss and review floor plans that are a reflection of your personal taste, but will still retain their value in the future."

In Conclusion

What are you waiting for? You hold in your hands the key to unlocking tremendous personal power. You can do, be or have anything you want. Your limits are self-imposed constraints you set upon yourself. Dare to think big thoughts and dream big dreams. Break out of your comfort zone, get in the game and run to win. Make your plan, work your plan with persistence and you will achieve the life you so richly deserve. Plan *now* to achieve what others only dare to dream.

Index

R

Real estate, partners in 40

Red herring 97

Reduction to the ridiculous
close 70

Resale homes 48

Resort and retirement
communities, qualifying for
29

S

Scripts for negotiating 107

Selling without completed
homes 48

Silence 95

Strategy, establishing the 108

Summary close 68

Four-step process to develop
your 68

T

Take it or leave it close 73

Tie-down words, list of 63

Tie-downs, types of 64

Time frame, qualifying 30

Trade off, the 101

Trial balloon 100

Trial close 64

Trial closes to memorize 65

Trial closing questions 51

Types of neighbors who live in
the community, prospect
questions the 44

U

Unfinished models,
demonstrating 45

V

View the model homes
unattended, prospect wants
to 43

Vise, the 99

W

Wants, needs and desires,
qualifying 35

Wince, the 95

Y

Yard 47

Year round homes, qualifying
for 28

Yes momentum close 63

Myers Barnes

is an acknowledged trendsetter in global new home sales and is known worldwide as one of the home building industry's most significant authorities in new home sales training, management, marketing, and real estate consulting.

Myers is the ultimate business advisor for today's home building and industry leaders, and is the best-selling author of numerous books specializing in new home sales training. His New Home Sales Training and New Home Sales Management seminars are the premier training events of the home building industry.

Start your journey toward New Home Sales Super-Achievement Today! Visit www.MyersBarnes.com to discover training videos, resources for sales professionals, and cutting-edge strategies for new home sales success.

 *Watch me on YouTube at **YouTube.com/MyersBarnes***

 *Follow me on Twitter at **Twitter.com/MyersBarnes***

 *Visit me on Facebook at **Facebook.com/NewHomeSalesTraining***

 *Discover all the new home sales resources at **MyersBarnes.com** or call **(252) 261-7611** for more information.*

The Myers Barnes Associates Evolutionary Profitability Program

Myers Barnes Associates is bringing breakthrough innovations and solutions to every homebuilder in America with the *Evolutionary Profitability Program*. Our mission: help you generate substantial profits. The way we accomplish this is to provide your team with actionable methods and strategies that will grow your business.

Identify your organization's strengths and weaknesses; clarify your vision; sharpen your long-term focus; and provide a personalized process that aligns your mission, vision, strategies and day-to-day operations—in an age of rapid change and upheaval, the Evolutionary Profitability Program provides stability and guidance through the peaks and pitfalls of growth while you reinvent your company.

Implementing the Myers Barnes Associates Evolutionary Profitability Program will allow You to Achieve:

- Controlled, Sustainable Growth and Expansion
- Improved Profitability, Financial Management and Customer Retention
- Systemic Personnel Recruitment
- Talent Development
- Systems and Process Integration
- Effective Policies and Procedures
- Management and Leadership Coaching
- Regularly Scheduled Educational Programs
- A Sustained Competitive Advantage
- Unparalleled Customer Service

Turn challenges into breakthrough opportunities with Myers Barnes Associates. Visit www.MyersBarnes.com or call (252) 261-7611.

MYERS BARNES ASSOCIATES, INC.

MyersBarnes.com

A Comprehensive Online Resource for New Home Sales Professionals

MyersBarnes.com is a trusted repository of tactics, strategy, and wisdom, as well as a place where likeminded professionals can connect and share their thoughts. There you'll find social media connections, training videos, an incredibly informative blog, and many more critically important resources for new home sales professionals. If "good enough" isn't good enough for you, you'll find the tools you need to become truly exceptional at www.MyersBarnes.com.

ResourceCenter »
Truly valuable tools, tested strategies, & innovative approaches with proven results.

PrivateTraining »
Pump up your bottom line & increase your sales performance.

MyersBlog »
Learn about & contribute to the latest New Home Sales strategies.

MYERS BARNES ASSOCIATES, INC.

The Fundamentals of Real Estate Marketing Have

Changed Forever

NDG Communications is the results-focused interactive and advertising agency, founded on the principles of the new media revolution. NDG Communications delivers real results for developers, builders, and realtors.

Get the tools, guidance, and innovation your company needs to succeed online at NDGcommunications.com.

 NDG will multiply the effectiveness of your advertising and marketing and create totally new concepts because their eyes are on the future. NDG's work will take you to the promised land.

MYERS BARNES, MYERS BARNES & ASSOCIATES

NDG Communications, Inc.

Visit our blog at **NDGcommunications.com/blog**, watch us on YouTube, or join us on Facebook.

NOTES

NOTES

NOTES

NOTES

 **MYERS BARNES** ASSOCIATES, INC.

Myers Barnes, America's Favorite New Home Sales Educator, Teaches Successful Salespeople the Tools They Need to Become Bulletproof in Any Real Estate Market

Widely regarded as the authority on new home sales, Myers Barnes has helped generate billions of dollars in revenue for builders, developers, and top corporations. Myers Barnes can teach you the most important and effective sales strategies and techniques in the new home sales industry.

Learn and Live the Difference Between Merely Surviving and Truly Thriving!

*FREE Training Videos available on YouTube and **MyersBarnes.com***

 *Watch me on YouTube at **YouTube.com/MyersBarnes***

 *Follow me on Twitter at **Twitter.com/MyersBarnes***

 *Visit me on Facebook at **Facebook.com/NewHomeSalesTraining***

 *Discover all the new home sales resources at **MyersBarnes.com** or call **(252) 261-7611** for more information.*